STUDIES IN MINISTRY AND WORSHIP

EDITORS: G. W. H. LAMPE & DAVID M. PATON

WHAT IS LITURGICAL PREACHING?

What is Liturgical Preaching?

REGINALD H. FULLER

*Professor of New Testament Literature and Languages
at Seabury-Western Theological Seminary,
Evanston, Illinois, U.S.A.*

SCM PRESS LTD
56 BLOOMSBURY STREET
LONDON

First published 1957
Reprinted 1960

Printed in Great Britain by
The Camelot Press Ltd., London and Southampton

CONTENTS

5

VIRO VENERABILI JOHANNI OLDCASTLE COBHAM

ARCHIDIACONO NUNC DUNELMENSI

PRINCIPI OLIM COLLEGII REGINAE

BIRMINGHAMENSIS

QUI ME IN DISCIPLINIS VEL LITURGICIS

IUVENEM INSTRUXIT

VEL HOMILETICIS

PREFACE TO THE SECOND EDITION

A few slight corrections, additions, omissions and modifications have been made to the text of this book as printed in the first (1957) edition.

The major criticism of the first edition was that I was too complacently attached to the liturgy of 1662, and that in particular I advocated the retention of the Lord's Prayer in its anomalous position after the communion of the people. In fact, however, I was not discussing the pros and cons of revision at all, but placing myself in the position of a parish priest who uses a given rite, and has in his sermon to relate the Biblical message to that rite. Since 1955 I have used another (viz., the American) rite, in which the *Our Father* comes before the communion. In this context the same point can be made, though in a different way: The *Our* Father is introduced with the words 'And now, as our Saviour Christ hath taught us, we are bold to say'. To call God Father is therefore an *audacious* act, which we can only presume to do 'now', namely when we have recalled before him the saving passion and resurrection of the Son as the sole ground of our acceptance. I have elsewhere (*Anglican Theological Review*, July, 1959) demonstrated, I hope, an abundant concern for liturgical revision. We have to learn to combine a desire for revision with a loyal use and patient endeavour to understand the liturgy that we have. The individual parish priest has no more right to criticize the existing liturgy from the pulpit than he has to make unauthorized revisions of his own in its performance.

Evanston, Illinois　　　　　　　　　　　　　　　　　　　　R.H.F.
October 1960

WHAT IS LITURGICAL PREACHING?

I. INTRODUCTION: GIVING OR GETTING?

IT has become almost a commonplace in Anglican circles to-day to proclaim from the pulpit that people come to church not to get, but to give. By that it is meant that they do not come to hear the sermon. Often it is even suggested that the inclusion of a sermon in the service at all is simply a grudging concession to the whims of the laity. To come to church to get is held up as something which only benighted Nonconformists do, and therefore inherently perverse and 'uncatholic'. It is man-centred, humanistic, subjective. To come to church to give, to offer, on the other hand, is 'Catholic', and therefore wholly right and proper. It is God-centred and objective.

One suspects, however, that behind this ostensible, and often ostentatious, devotion to what is supposed to be 'Catholicism' there lurks in the background something far more sinister. For what if it be, not Catholicism, but—British Pelagianism? What if man has nothing to give? What if all our righteousnesses are as filthy rags? Wherewith shall we come before the Most High? Surely, not trusting in our own righteousness, but only in God's manifold and great mercies. So before we can give—and in the end, of course, worship *is* giving—we must get. We must get that righteousness which is by faith, that righteousness which is Christ himself. Only then can we give. Only then can we offer the one acceptable sacrifice to God, the sacrifice of Christ himself, and ourselves as found only in him. Worship is a two-way traffic. It is not one-way traffic from heaven to earth, as certain kinds of Protestantism have held (and here the Anglican protest is legitimate, though one-sided), nor one-way traffic from earth to heaven. Worship we repeat is a two-way traffic. In worship we behold the angels of God ascending and descending upon the Son of Man.

9

Surprising, and even shocking though it may seem to many, Luther was on the right lines here. Confronted with the mediaeval Mass, conceived as it was in terms of a one-way traffic from earth to heaven, Luther insisted the essence of worship was the sermon and the response of the congregation,[1] and reformed the Church's liturgy in accordance with this insight. Unfortunately, however, he placed the congregation's response, not where it was intended to be, *viz*. in the liturgical action, but in the singing of the chorale. As a result, the liturgical tradition was so whittled down in the Lutheran Churches[2] that in Germany it became in the end little more than a recitation of the words of institution as a prelude to communion. The people, having received the Word in the sermon, and having responded to that Word in the chorale, receive the sacrament as a confirmatory appendage to the sermon.[3]

II. SERMONS WITHOUT LITURGY

Unfortunately, when the sermon is divorced from its proper context in the liturgical action, preaching degenerates in one or other of three directions. It becomes intellectualism, moralism or emotionalism. We have had the first in seventeenth-century Lutheran orthodoxy, the second in Tillotsonian Anglicanism,[4] and the third in the pietism of all the Protestant Churches, Anglican Evangelicalism included. In the arid intellectualism of orthodoxy the preacher had the quite laudable aim of conveying sound doctrine to the minds of his hearers and of securing their intellectual

[1] See 'Luther and Public Worship', by Toive Harjumpää in *Luther Speaks*. Essays by Lutheran Pastors, 1947, pp. 47-54.

[2] See Yngve Brilioth, *Eucharistic Faith and Practice, Catholic and Evangelical*, 1930, pp. 144-52.

[3] Lest my Lutheran friends should think this too sweeping, I may mention that I attended a Lutheran *Abendmahl* in Germany in 1951 at which there was a forty-five minute sermon, and for lack of time the pastor merely recited the Words of Institution, followed by Communion, the latter part of the service taking only ten minutes!

[4] For Tillotson and his preaching see Charles Smyth, *The Art of Preaching 747-1939*, 1940, Chap. IV.

assent. But he did not thereby produce an *ecclesia*, a congregation. In moralistic preaching the preacher appealed to the wills of his hearers. He produced, once more not an ecclesia, a congregation, but, if his words fell on good soil, moral individuals. And the emotional preacher may succeed in producing all kinds of spiritual excitement, even, as in the Welsh revivals, glossolalia. But as St Paul remarked long ago, glossolalia does not 'edify', nor do other kinds of spiritual excitement. They do not build up (*oikodomein*) the Church. All three kinds of preaching are individualistic. They leave a man in his isolation. They do not draw him anew into the *ecclesia*. For unless the sermon leads to the liturgical action the *ecclesia* does not go on to express itself as the *ecclesia*. The individual may be 'edified' in the popular, non-biblical sense of the word. But he still goes home as an individual; a better person, we hope, intellectually, morally and emotionally, but still an individual. Hymn singing may foster a sense of community, as Luther apparently realized (and as a notable Congregationalist layman has observed, hymns *are* the dissenter's liturgy). Hymns, in Nonconformity, have served to keep alive a full-blooded presentation of the Gospel and a genuine self-understanding of the *ecclesia* at a time when the preaching and the extemporary prayers have presented a humanistic or humanitarian substitute for the Gospel. What people sing makes a more lasting impression on their minds, especially by frequent repetition, than what they hear, and if there is a disparity between what they hear and what they sing, what they sing will win in the long run. In this way hymns (especially the hymns of Watts and Wesley[1]) have functioned much in the same way as the liturgy of the Book of Common Prayer which, as Dr Reinhold Niebuhr has somewhere remarked, has kept alive an Augustinian presentation of the Gospel during times when Anglican pulpits have preached Pelagianism.

So much is doubtless proved by the singing of 'Abide with me' or *Cwm Rhondda* at a football match. Yet the Cup Final may

[1] See Bernard L. Manning in *The Hymns of Wesley and Watts*, 1942.

serve to remind us that hymn-singing, like patriotism, is not enough! Much of course depends on the content of the hymn. It is all-important that the congregation's response to the Word of God should be the response of the *ecclesia* at the deepest level of her being. If the hymn is sufficiently objective and kerygmatic, if it expresses the great classical truths of our redemption, it can go a long way towards achieving this. That is notably the case with the Passion Chorales of J. S. Bach. But hymns do not of themselves enable the Church to *act* as such, and it is of the essence of liturgy that in it the Church *acts* in a manner expressive of her deepest being. Hymns, in their Anglican use, serve the very useful purpose of *commenting* on the liturgy, reinforcing and driving home what is being done in the liturgy. But they are no adequate substitute for the liturgy itself.

The purpose of the liturgical sermon is to renew in the individual members the sense that they are members of the *ecclesia*, constituted as such by the redemptive act of God in Christ. The sermon—as we shall see later—acts as a bridge between Baptism and the Eucharist. As Dr Karl Barth has observed,[1] 'Baptism and the Lord's Supper form what we may call the natural bounds of the church service.' In the chief Eucharist of the ancient Church's year, the great paschal Eucharist which was the norm of all the others, the service started with the Baptism of the catechumens and culminated in the Lord's Supper. On other occasions, when Baptism is not administered, it is the function of the liturgical sermon to reach back to the Baptism of the members of the congregation, to renew in them the sense of membership of the ecclesia, and to lead forward to the liturgical action of the Eucharist. Baptism is the ground of the Church's existence,[2] the Eucharist is the ground of her continuance.

The service therefore which has a sermon but no liturgy, the service which culminates in a sermon related neither backward

---

[1] Karl Barth, *The Knowledge of God and the Service of God*, 1938, p. 211. Cf. also pp. 194-8.
[2] Karl Barth, *op. cit.*, p. 195.

to Baptism nor forward to the Eucharist is, as Karl Barth has rightly observed,[1] a 'torso'. If modern educationists insist on the importance of 'expression work' in teaching, how much more important is expression work in the church service!

III. LITURGY WITHOUT SERMON

But what about the service in which there is liturgy without sermon? Is that, as Karl Barth no less vigorously insists, equally a torso? The reader will remember the energy with which Richard Hooker resisted the Puritan demand for a sermon at every service.[2] The Puritans maintained that it was only when the Word of God was preached from the pulpit that it became audible to the assembled congregation. Hooker agrees that the hearing of the Word of God is an integral and essential part of Christian worship. But he goes on to argue that the reading of scripture by itself, without a sermon, can in fact be a proclamation of the Word. When the scriptures are read in the public service (no doubt Hooker is thinking of weekday Morning and Evening Prayer, since the sermon was prescribed at the Sunday morning service, and the children were to be catechized before Evening Prayer on Sunday afternoons), the congregation *can* hear the Word of God in the lections without the necessity of a sermon. We must surely agree with Hooker that often the bare reading of scripture (particularly when the reading of it is taken seriously as part of the ministry of the Word) can be a real proclamation of the Word. And our modern Anglican practice of celebrating the Holy Communion without a sermon, although contrary to the rubric, does not necessarily silence the Word, since the Epistle and Gospel are invariably read.

[1] Karl Barth, *op. cit.*, p. 211: 'What we know today as the church service both in Roman Catholicism *and* in Protestantism is a torso. The Roman Catholic Church has a sacramental service without preaching. But I wish to speak at the moment not for or against her, but about our own Protestant Church. We have a service with a sermon but without sacraments. Both types of service are impossible.'

[2] R. Hooker, *Eccles. Pol.* V. 22.

IV. THE AIM OF LITURGICAL PREACHING

We will grant, then, that while the reading of the scriptures may often of itself be a sufficient proclamation of the Word, without which there can be no worship at all in the Christian sense of response to the mighty acts of God in Jesus Christ, yet the effectiveness of such proclamation without sermon depends upon the regular preaching of the sermon at the chief service of the week, as the Book of Common Prayer plainly requires.

But why does the Prayer Book make this requirement? Why should there be a sermon? The obvious answer is that many parts of scripture are difficult to understand, and that, like the Ethiopian eunuch (Acts 8.30-1), we need one more competent than ourselves to explain its meaning to us. There is a modicum of truth in this. Unless we have made the Bible a subject of prolonged study and are familiar with its theology, we are bound to find much of it beyond our comprehension. Yet if that were the sole aim of preaching, it would be the preacher's task ultimately to render himself dispensable. It would then be theoretically possible for a congregation to progress sufficiently in the knowledge of the scriptures that it would no longer require their exegesis in a sermon. Like the parent, the schoolteacher and the doctor, the preacher's task would be to make himself superfluous. The child grows to manhood, the scholar passes his General School Certificate, and the patient recovers his health. Moreover, if this were the sole motive of preaching, the preacher would be confronted with the difficulty occasioned by the varying degrees of intellectual capacity, spiritual experience and biblical knowledge among the members of his congregation. For some the sermon would still be necessary, for others it would be a mere waste of time. The farm labourer, the housewife and the office boy might have to listen attentively, while the saint and the professor of theology could compose themselves for twenty minutes' slumber, or worse still, listen simply in order to criticize the preacher! But the sermon is addressed to the whole body of the faithful with the intention of producing the same response in all, young and old, simple and learned alike. The place for scriptural exegesis is in Sunday schools, Church tutorial classes, and in private admonitions 'as well to the sick as to the whole': their place in the sermon is only incidental. On such non-liturgical occasions the explanations of the difficulties of scripture can be adapted to the needs of the individual or the group concerned, and to the level of their intellectual, moral and spiritual attainments.

Others will see the *raison d'être* of the sermon in the fact that whereas the scriptures speak to a situation in the past, the preacher's function is to bring the word of scripture out of the past and to relate it to the needs of his congregation. Once more, it would be wrong to underestimate the value of the sermon in doing this. There will always be some who on any given Sunday can come out of church saying: 'The Vicar knew just what I needed: it was just as though he was speaking to me personally.' All preachers will gratefully acknowledge those occasions when some member of the congregation has thanked them for their 'message'. But this can never be the sole, nor even the main purpose of the sermon. Although frequent pastoral visitation will familiarize the parish priest with the needs and problems of his flock, particularly in the country, where the parish is of manageable compass, he can never hope to satisfy the needs of all his people all the time. And if that is what they are looking for, there will always be many who go home saying that the sermon contained no 'message' for them; that particular sermon is written off as far as they are concerned. Again, the proper place for such personal administrations is in 'private admonitions, as well to the sick as to the whole'. If the primary purpose of the sermon is to satisfy the needs of the individual in this way, it would always be open to anyone to argue that there was no point in his going to church at all, since the Vicar never has any message for him! Above all, such a conception of the purpose of preaching reduces the liturgy to the level of a mere introduction, as a North of

Ireland journalist thought when he reported a church service in a local newspaper in the following terms: 'The Curate having finished the preliminaries, the Rector delivered himself of an eloquent discourse' (!).

There is much talk nowadays, especially on the other side of the Atlantic, about 'preaching to people's needs'. A popular American book, which indicates a whole philosophy of preaching, is entitled *Man's Need and God's Action*. The supreme test to which the Gospel and its preaching is put is: 'Is it (not true, but) relevant?' Indeed, we might almost say that we live in an age which is marked by a cult of the relevant. This cult, which began in the humanistic liberal period, is apparently cashing in at the moment on the present lively interest in existentialism, with its emphasis on the Kierkegaardian principle that 'truth is subjectivity'. A statement is not true unless it can be made true to me. And it cannot be made true to me unless it can be shown to concern my existence and has an answer to the problems it poses. Now of course the existentialists are uttering a salutary warning against 'false objectivity'. The gospel is not being preached at all if it is preached as an abstraction right over the heads of the congregation. For the highest response which such preaching can hope for is an intellectual acceptance of a formalistic kind. Faith, however, is the acceptance of the events of redemption as events that have occurred *'pro nobis'*. But the preoccupation with what can be shown to be immediately and directly relevant is perhaps even more dangerous. For the gospel is concerned with man's *ultimate* needs, with his need for forgiveness and redemption. Men and women are usually conscious of their less-than-ultimate needs, their need for security, for deliverance from anxiety and frustration, for the attainment of social acceptance and the like—in fact, all the things which drive the bourgeoisie to assemble themselves in troupes at the psychiatrist's consulting-rooms. In this situation the Church is tempted to compete with the psychiatrists on their own level, and to offer people the kind of 'comfort' they are looking for in these less-than-ultimate needs. In doing this, however, the Church is trimming down the gospel to the measure of these needs. No doubt the Galatian Judaizers were offering a gospel more immediately satisfying to the needs of the Galatians than St Paul's gospel. But that was the supreme danger: 'Though we or an angel from heaven should preach unto you, let him be anathema.' Much so-called 'relevant' preaching comes under that anathema. Our chief concern must be, not the people's needs but the gospel in its fullness. This gospel may come first to expose their needs as trivial and even false, revealing to them for the first time what they had as yet scarce dreamed of, that they have an ultimate need, a need which is only exposed when they stand naked at the 'last day' before the judgement seat of God. Penultimate needs will otherwise lead to penultimate comforts. The comfort of the Gospel is available only on the other side of judgement.

There is a third conception of preaching which is by no means rare. This takes the line that the sermon is comparable to the type of public speaking which takes place at the annual festal gathering of a society or club. The speaker is probably himself a member of the society, and he delivers a eulogy on its objects and achievements—all of which are familiar enough already to his audience, of course. One member is chosen to do this since all cannot speak at once, and all are perhaps not sufficiently eloquent or capable of expressing their thoughts intelligibly. They listen to one who acts as their mouthpiece, a better speaker with the training and experience to formulate their own inarticulate thoughts. They listen not to new information, but to what they know, implicitly at least, already, but could not frame for themselves. Is that the purpose of the sermon? Is it simply the articulate expression of the religious experience already latent in the congregation? Such, at any rate, was Schleiermacher's view,[1]

[1] F. Schleiermacher, *Praktische Theologie*, p. 239: 'We must treat our congregation as people who are already Christians, not as people who want to become so.' Cf. also his *Studien und Kritiken*, 1829, p. 267: 'We must not suppose that we are bringing to our congregations something new.' (Quoted by Karl Fezer, *Das Wort Gottes und die Predigt*, 1925, pp. 39f.)

B

a view which seems to have been not without influence in pietistic circles in Britain, especially in Wales, where the Deacons in the Big Seat punctuate the delivery of the sermon with alleluias, praise be's and ayes, and groanings that cannot be uttered. They know it all already, their own experience is commensurate with the preacher's, and they can assent to everything he says. But it is just not true that all the members of the congregation are of equal spiritual maturity. Such preaching is bound to be addressed to the spiritual élite, treating the Big Seat as though it were the whole of the congregation. Thus it leads to the diametrically opposite error to the merely instructional view of preaching. But the Church of Jesus Christ contains both wheat and tares. *All* Christians, even the most spiritually advanced, are sinners. All come to church as the poor in spirit, who hunger and thirst after righteousness. They come, not to be confronted by themselves, but by the judgement and grace of God. A sermon may be comforting, but it may be just as properly disturbing.

None of the foregoing conceptions of preaching can justify the integral place of the sermon in the liturgy. If that place is to be justified, the sermon must bear an integral relation both to the reading of the scriptures which precedes it, and to the eucharistic offering which follows it.

V. THE SERVICE OF THE WORD AS AN INTEGRAL PART OF THE EUCHARIST

Before we proceed to the main topic of this section, it is necessary first to consider the place of the scriptural lections in the liturgy. It is widely held[1] that the service of the Word was originally held at a separate gathering distinct from the assembly of

---

[1] E.g. Gregory Dix, *The Shape of the Liturgy*, 1944, p. 36, etc., and (with a characteristic greater degree of caution) J. H. Srawley, *The Early History of the Liturgy*, 1949, second edition, p. 34. Srawley inclines to the opinion that 'some of the elements' of the synagogue service 'were associated quite early, if not from the first, with the Christian sacred meal'.

the *ecclesia* for the Eucharist proper (the so-called *synaxis*), and that it was only gradually, and for reasons of practical convenience, that the two services were eventually fused. If such were the case, it would follow that there are no historical reasons for believing the service of the Word to be an integral part of the eucharistic celebration. But a different view of worship in the early Church has been propounded by Dr Cullmann.[1] The description of the Church's corporate activities in Acts 2.42, he maintains, suggests that the apostles' teaching, or ministry of the Word, the prayers (presumably the Church's intercessions and the great eucharistic prayer) and the breaking of the bread were all integral parts of the one service. This, he claims, is supported by the earliest description of an actual Eucharist we possess, in Acts 20.7ff., where St Paul is stated to have discoursed at great length before breaking the bread.[2] There is further evidence in the New Testament which seems to bear out Dr Cullmann's suggestion. First, St Paul's discussion of glossolalia in I Cor. 14 suggests that preaching (verse 13), praying (verse 14) and the giving of thanks (i.e. the great eucharistic prayer, verse 16) were the regular features of the church gathering *in that order*. Moreover, it seems that the Pauline epistles were not only intended to be read at the gatherings of the community, but were actually so framed as to lead into the performance of the liturgy.[3] The conclusion of I Corinthians offers the clearest indication of this, for it consists of a number of phrases suggestive of a transition from the epistle itself to a celebration of the Eucharist: 'Salute one another with a holy kiss' (=the kiss of peace immediately preceding (the *Sursum Corda* and?) the prayer of thanksgiving); 'if any man love not the Lord, let him be anathema' (cf. Didache 10.6 and the *hagia tois hagiois* of the later liturgies); '*marana tha*'

---

[1] *Early Christian Worship*, 1953, p. 12.

[2] I am informed by Dr H.-C. Schmidt of Hamburg that certain Benedictine liturgical scholars in Germany agree with Cullmann's implied criticism of Dix on this point.

[3] I Cor. 16.22-4. See the article by John A. T. Robinson in *JTS*, n.s. Vol. IV, Pt. I, pp. 38-41.

(a petition for the coming of Christ in the Communion in anticipation of the Parousia, or as the Rev. A. H. Couratin has suggested to me, as the true Celebrant of the Eucharist);[1] 'the grace
of the Lord Jesus Christ be with you all' (=the salutation intro-
ducing the dialogue before the prayer of thanksgiving). It would
seem therefore that the instances adduced by Dix of 'survivals'
of a Eucharist without preceding *synaxis* (viz. the baptismal
Eucharist in Justin Martyr's *Apology*, the ordination Eucharist
in Hippolytus' *Apostolic Tradition*, and the Maundy Thursday
celebration of later times[2]) are not survivals, but *exceptions* from
the norm explicable on other grounds.

Furthermore, recent continental studies[3] seem to have proved,
contrary to generally received opinion in Britain, that the Last
Supper, if not the actual passover of that year, was probably at
least an anticipation of the passover. Now the passover was invariably preceded by the *haggada*, a discourse relating the meal
and its elements to the saving events of the Exodus. Before
thanks was offered to God for the mighty acts of the Exodus, the
participants must have those events brought to mind. Thus the
passover would seem to have been a memorial in a double sense
—a memorial to man, *and* a memorial before God, the first taking
place in the *haggada*, and the second in the *berakoth* or prayers
of blessing recited over the elements. This perhaps throws light
on the vexed question of the meaning of *anamnesis* in I Cor.

[1] See J. Jeremias, *The Eucharistic Words of Jesus*, 1955, p. 164.
O. Cullmann, *op. cit.*, p. 16, and cf. Didache, *loc. cit.*

[2] Gregory Dix, *op. cit.*, p. 36.

[3] Jeremias (*op. cit.*) has conclusively disposed of the usual alternative
suggestions to a passover meal (sabbath-*kiddush*, passover *kiddush*,
chaburah), though his own attempt to prove that Mark is historically
correct in his view that it was an actual passover is less convincing
(cf. V. Taylor, *St Mark*, 1952, pp. 664-7, who shrewdly remarks that
Jeremias' repeated attempts to explain away the residual difficulties of
the Markan chronology from Rabbinic exceptions 'wear thin'. In my
Mission and Achievement of Jesus, 1954, pp. 70f., I have fallen back on
the view of Théo Preiss that the Last Supper was an anticipated passover.).

11.24f.[1] The results of linguistic investigations on this subject are singularly inconclusive, and depend largely on the presuppositions of the investigator, who nearly always has a 'Protestant' or a 'Catholic' axe to grind. If the matrix of the Christian Eucharist was the Jewish passover, then it must be a memorial in the same double sense as the passover, judged by what actually happened at the rite, must have been. As the passover began with the *haggada*, which recalled the saving events of the Exodus and brought them to the minds of the participants, so the service of the Word in the Christian dispensation will recall the saving events of Jesus Christ before the congregation. But this recalling before man is the preliminary to the recalling of the events before God by way of eucharistic recital, so that God in turn may make those events actually present to the participants. The service of the Word, like the passover *haggada*, relates the second part of the service to the redemptive events of the past, without which the Godward act would be meaningless. Unless the Eucharist proper is preceded by the ministry of the Word, the liturgy becomes a Pelagian affair, a work of man, a purely human offering. It is then an arrogant attempt of man to storm the heights of heaven and to establish communion with God for himself. This would reduce the liturgy to the status of a mystery cult, to what St Paul and St John would have stigmatized as *sarx*, flesh, which profiteth nothing. If the mighty acts of God in Christ are to become the stuff of Christian worship, stuff for recital before God in thanksgiving—and it is this, and this alone, which

[1] Recent Protestant exegesis, while recognizing the dynamic nature of *anamnesis*, in the sense that it brings a past event into the present as an objective reality, contends that it is a manward act. See, e.g., W. C. van Unnik in *Niederlandsch Theologisch Tijdschrift*, August 1950, followed by A. J. B. Higgins, *The Lord's Supper in the New Testament*, 1952; W. M. F. Scott in Theology, February 1952, pp. 42ff., and, in subsequent correspondence, June 1953, pp. 222ff.; October 1953, pp. 385ff. Also an article by Douglas Jones, *JTS*, Vol. VI, part 2, pp. 183-91. The 'Catholic' view (also upheld by several Lutherans) is that it is a Godward act, though this is variously conceived. See, e.g., Dix, *op. cit.*, pp. 161f., etc.; J. Jeremias, *op. cit.*, pp. 115ff.; P. Brunner in *Leiturgia*, Vol. I, 1954, pp. 210-214, 229-232.

distinguishes Christian worship from pagan—; if the only way to worship God 'in spirit and in truth' is to come before him rehearsing these mighty acts, then the congregation must first be confronted anew with these same mighty acts, before it can make them the material of its worship. That is why the Church from its earliest days has preceded the Eucharist proper with the service of the Word.

There are three types of ministry of the Word, at least, discernible in the New Testament. There is *kerygma*, missionary preaching to the unconverted. There is *paraklesis*, a renewal and deepening of the apprehension of the *kerygma* in the already converted, and *didache*, the instruction of the new converts and of the already baptized in Christian ethics and doctrine.[1] It will be well for us to keep these distinctions in mind in what follows. In speaking of 'liturgical preaching' we are dealing with a type of preaching which conforms to *paraklesis* in the New Testament classification.[2]

VI. THE SERMON AS A NORMAL PART OF
THE SERVICE OF THE WORD

We are now in a position to answer the question, Why is the sermon needed, as well as the reading of scripture? For the purpose of the sermon is to extract from the scripture readings the essential core and content of the gospel, to penetrate behind the day's pericope to the proclamation of the central act of God in Christ which it contains, in order that the central act of God can be made the material for recital in the prayer of thanksgiving.

It is just here that the more recent phases of modern critical scholarship can be of inestimable help to the pastor and parish

---

[1] See Bo Reicke, 'A Synopsis of Early Christian Preaching' in *The Root of the Vine*, by A. Friedrichsen and others, 1953, pp. 132-53.

[2] The Epistle to the Hebrews is a *logos parakleseōs* (Heb. 13.22): it may be regarded as a single expository liturgical sermon or as a series of such sermons, plus an epistolary ending and other modifications.

priest. For recent scholarship has demonstrated anew the fundamental unity of the New Testament. This unity lies in the *kerygma*,
the proclamation of the central acts of God's redemption in Jesus
Christ. This proclamation, which underlies every part of the New
Testament and gives it its unity, has been summarized as follows:[1]

> The prophecies are fulfilled, and the new Age is inaugurated
>   by the coming of Christ
>
> He was born of the seed of David.
>
> He died according to the Scriptures, to deliver us out of this
>   present evil age.
>
> He was buried.
>
> He rose on the third day according to the Scriptures.
>
> He is exalted at the right hand of God, as the Son of God and
>   Lord of the quick and dead.
>
> He will come again as Judge and Saviour of men.

This *kerygma* is not a bare series of historical statements and pre-
dictions, nor is it a series of metaphysical propositions. It is the
proclamation of an event and a person, of the event and person
who is Jesus Christ, the eschatological redemptive act of God.
And the aim of that proclamation is not to secure intellectual
assent to the statements it enshrines, but to evoke faith, faith
which is personal encounter with the person proclaimed, and
acceptance of the event he is as that which God has wrought
pro nobis.

Now the New Testament, roughly speaking, consists of two
halves, the Epistles and the Gospels. Both parts have their origin
in the *kerygma* as summarized above; and both, in different
ways, are expansions and therefore expressions of the *kerygma*.

VII. LITURGICAL PREACHING

(*a*) THE EPISTLES

The epistles are addressed to those who have already accepted

[1] Quoted from C. H. Dodd, *The Apostolic Preaching and its Developments*, 1944, Second edition, p. 17.

the apostolic preaching of Jesus Christ as the redemptive act of God—see, for instance, I Thess. 1.5ff. They assume a knowledge of this preaching, and proceed to expound its doctrinal and ethical implications. The doctrinal portions of the epistles are not a series of revealed propositional statements, nor flights of speculative imagination.[1] They are rather attempts to draw out the implications for thought of the encounter with Christ mediated by the *kerygma*. A perspicuous example of this is the way in which St Paul deals with the problems raised by the Corinthians in connexion with the resurrection. He answers their questions, not by formulating propositions derived from an original deposit of revealed truths, nor by speculations of his own, but by citing the relevant parts of the preaching he had originally delivered to them and deducing therefrom its implications for the problem in hand (I Cor. 15.3ff.). In the same way, the ethical exhortations or paraenetic sections of the epistles are not a series of categorical imperatives revealed from heaven, nor ethical ideals evolved by the speculative imagination of the Apostle. Rather, they spring immediately out of the new relation into which his converts have been brought with the event of Jesus Christ as a result of their hearing of the preaching and baptism. As an instance we may cite St Paul's treatment of slavery. He does not lay down a regulation that all slaves are forthwith to be emancipated, nor does he speculate about their 'rights' in the abstract. He starts instead with the new relation to God into which they have been brought through the *kerygma* in Christ. Their service to their earthly masters is thus seen as a parable and a means of their service to God in Christ. Similarly, the treatment of slaves by their masters is controlled by the masters' knowledge that they too have a Master: 'Saint Paul insisted that all men, masters and slaves alike, are called to entire obedience to Christ who has purchased them as a slave was purchased into freedom, but by a real, instead of a fictitious, act of redemption.'[2] Nor is this

---

[1] Cf. John A. T. Robinson, *In the End God*, 1950, pp. 25ff.
[2] F. N. Davey, *The Word of Testimony*, 1951, p. 21.

23729

pattern of ethical paraenesis peculiar to the Pauline epistles. The author of I Peter paints his injunctions to slaves on an even more explicit Christological canvas. The Christian slave reproduces in his own behaviour the pattern of Christ's deportment in his passion as the Suffering Servant, bearing our sins in his own body on the tree (I Pet. 2.8-25). A consideration of the duties of slaves thus leads the author to heart of the *kerygma* of Christ's atoning death. Here is no flat moralism, dogmatic or speculative, but an ethic springing direct from the redemptive act of God in Christ and its proclamation in the *kerygma*.

All this suggests the lines on which the liturgical Epistle for the Day will be treated in the liturgical sermon. If the Epistle is taken from the doctrinal portion of the epistles, the preacher's task will be to penetrate behind the doctrinal argumentation to the *kerygma* whose implications are being set forth, and to confront the congregation with that *kerygma* so that they might renew their response to it in faith, preparatory to the Godward memorial of the liturgical action. And the Epistles from the paraenetic sections will demand a similar treatment. They are not to be used for little moralistic exhortations of the preacher's own. His task is rather to penetrate behind the paraenesis to the *kerygma* it presupposes, to confront the congregation with that *kerygma* so that it may be the occasion of a renewed encounter with Jesus Christ in the liturgy and thence to indicate the kind of behaviour that encounter will imply in the daily lives of the people in their contemporary situation. This, incidentally, is why the New Testament is so disappointing as a handbook of Christian ethics, passing over as it does so many of the burning issues which beset the modern world. For 'Christian morality consists in giving effect within human relations to the divine charity which is the glory of God disclosed in the work of Christ'.[1] The ethical injunctions of the New Testament epistles are simply illustrations of the way in which that divine charity should operate in terms of human relations. It is the preacher's task to assist his

[1] C. H. Dodd, *The Gospel and the Law of Christ*, 1946, p. 16.

25

people to a renewed encounter with that divine charity, so that they in turn can give effect to it within their own personal relations.

It is now proposed to offer a few examples of this kind of treatment of the liturgical Epistles. These examples must not be regarded as skeleton sermons, nor even as suggestions of what should actually be said in the pulpit. They are merely indications of the preliminary theological spade work which has to be done before a sermon can be constructed.[1] Three examples will be drawn from doctrinal passages, and three examples of the ethical type will follow.

(i) DOCTRINAL EPISTLES:

1. *First example:* CHRISTMAS I: GAL. 4.1-7

St Paul is expounding the relation between the law and the gospel. These represent two successive periods in redemptive history, the one marked by slavery and bondage, the other by sonship and freedom. The decisive event which inaugurates the new era is the mission of the Son of God: 'God sent forth his Son, made of a woman, made under the law' (verse 4). This is the *kerygma* behind the theological argument—the entrance of the Son of God into the world of men that we might become sons of God by adoption and grace. This—the event of the Incarnation—is the mighty act which the preacher must proclaim today. Here, in the sermon, the manward *anamnesis* will take this particular form. Then in response the Church will proceed to rehearse this event before God in the Proper Preface for Christmastide: 'Because thou didst give Jesus Christ thine only Son to be born as at this time for us; who by the operation of the Holy Ghost was made very man of the substance of the Virgin Mary his Mother.' Then, in response to the Church's rehearsal of the event of the Incarnation, God sends forth his Son, now no

[1] The method of treatment in these examples is akin to that of the German Lutheran *Predigtmeditationen* (sermon meditations), though the examples given here have in view the special purpose of liturgical preaching.

26

longer a Babe at Bethlehem, but exalted at his right hand in glory, yet condescending, as he once condescended in the crib at his nativity, to come to us under the lowly forms of bread and wine. Thus our status of adopted sons, into which we entered at our baptism, is hereby renewed. God sends forth the Spirit of his Son into our hearts crying, 'Abba, Father'. This aspect of the communion—the renewal of our baptismal adoption as sons in the Son—is brought out in the 1662 Communion service, in which the people join with the priest saying 'Our Father . . .' only *after* they have received the sacrament. We are therefore no longer bondservants, no longer under the law. No longer is there laid upon us the impossible burden of winning our sonship by our own moral efforts. Rather, we are sons who receive their sonship as a gift from the hands of God. And if sons, then heirs. All this is assured to us in the communion, as the Prayer of Thanksgiving expresses it: 'Thou dost assure us thereby . . . that we . . . are also *heirs* through hope of thy everlasting kingdom.' And with the Blessing at the end of the service we are sent forth into the world to live the life of sons, the life of freedom.

2. *Second example:* PASSION SUNDAY: HEB. 9.11-15

The author of Hebrews is expounding the doctrine of Christ's High Priesthood. But this doctrine is neither a *revelatum* nor an essay in speculation. It is an exposition of the kerygmatic assertions that 'Christ died for our sins according to the scriptures' (I Cor. 15.3), and that he was exalted to the right hand of God (Mark 12.36 para.; Acts 2.24f.; Heb. 1.13). Implicit in the first of these statements in the proclamation is the idea that Christ died as the Servant (Isa. 42.1ff., 53.1ff.), and as such inaugurated the New Covenant (Isa. 42.6 with Jer. 31.31ff.). Implicit in the second statement, the language of which is derived from Ps. 110.1, is the idea that by his death and exaltation Christ became the High Priest after the order of Melchizedek (Ps. 110.4). Thus the death and exaltation of Christ are the fundamental kerygmatic facts behind the Epistle to the Hebrews and therefore behind the liturgical Epistle of this day. But just as St Paul sees that the outcome of the mission of the Son of God is our adoption as sons (see above, p. 26), so the author of Hebrews regards the death and exaltation of Christ as the inauguration of a new way of worship (the word 'serve' in verse 14 (*latreuein*) is a liturgical word, denoting the specific service of God in worship). Because he has removed our sins by his atoning death ('purged our conscience from dead works [=sins]', verse 14), he has made it possible for us to have real access to and communion with God in worship, such as was never possible under the Old Covenant, whose sacrifices could remove only the technical impurities of a ritual kind. Now the Church's Eucharist is precisely the concrete realization of that new way of worship inaugurated by the redemptive act of God in Christ. For in this service we come before God, not bringing any sacrifice of our own, but throwing ourselves back upon that sacrifice which Christ offered 'once for all' (*eph' hapax*, verse 12, for which compare the Prayer of Consecration in the Book of Common Prayer: 'His one oblation of himself *once* offered') as we rehearse the deed of Calvary before God. It is only then, when we have made the *anamnesis* of the once-for-all sacrifice which is Christ's death and exaltation, that we are privileged to enter into communion with God and have that access into his presence, which, as the author of Hebrews sees, is the end of worship.

3. *Third example:* TRINITY IV: ROM. 8.18-25

In the earlier Middle Ages in Northern Europe, as in the present Latin rite, the Sundays after Trinity were reckoned from Whit-Sunday as Sundays after Pentecost, an arrangement which is still reflected in many of the Epistles of this season. The Epistle for this Sunday is an instance of this, for it describes certain aspects of the life in the Spirit. After his exaltation, and as the outcome of his death, Jesus poured out his Spirit upon the Church (Acts 2.4, 33; John 7.39, 20.22), that eschatological Spirit with which he himself had been endowed during his ministry on earth (Mark

1.10; John 1.32f.; Acts 10.38). Thus the situation of the Church between Pentecost and the Parousia is analogous to the situation of her Lord during his incarnate life (cf. I John 4.7). To live in the age of the Spirit of the Age to Come already during this present age is to live a life of tension between present humiliation and the future glory which is nevertheless already enjoyed in part through our having the first fruits of the Spirit. The linking of this thought backwards to the moment of Baptism should present little difficulty, but the forward link to the Holy Communion is less obvious. Yet it seems that the primitive Church regarded the end of the eucharistic action precisely as her renewal in the Spirit. In the earliest surviving text of the eucharistic prayer[1] the Bishop, having rehearsed before God his mighty acts in the incarnation, passion, resurrection and ascension of Christ (a rehearsal which corresponds to the 'series of thanksgivings' in the Jewish *berakah*) goes on to pray that the Church might be renewed in Holy Spirit: 'And we pray that . . . thou wouldest grant to all thy saints who partake to be filled with (the) Holy Spirit' (a prayer which corresponds to the petititon following the series of thanksgivings in the Jewish *berakah*). Our present liturgy (1662) says little or nothing of the eschatological work of the Holy Spirit in the communion, and this perhaps must be reckoned as one of its most serious defects.[2] Yet the whole complex of ideas

---

[1] *The Apostolic Tradition of Hippolytus*, translated and edited by B. S. Easton, 1934, p. 36.

[2] What is needed is not an *epiklesis* in the technical sense, i.e. an invocation of the Spirit that he may descend upon the elements to convert them into the Body and Blood of Christ, a later conception which appears in the standard Eastern liturgies, nor even that he may consecrate them to be the Body and Blood of Christ 'in virtue, power and effect' (as in Non-Juring eucharistic theology, and thence in the Scottish liturgy of 1764 and in the Anglican revisions down to the proposed Book of 1928), but a petition that through receiving the sacrament the *ecclesia* might be renewed in the Holy Spirit. The petition for the Spirit's operation is rightly placed after the commemoration of the work of the Son, thus retaining the traditional Trinitarian structure: the address to the Father, recital of the redemption accomplished in the Son, and petition for the Spirit to extend that redemption in the present. This pattern corresponds to the structure of the Jewish *berakah* (address-thanksgiving-petition). Cf. also *Theology*, Vol. LVIII, No. 424, pp. 387f.

suggested by the phrase 'first fruits of the Spirit' is hinted at in three places. First, there is the clause in the Prayer of Consecration: 'Until his coming again,' suggesting as it does that the Holy Communion belongs to the interim time between the two comings of Christ, the time characterized by the dispensation of the Spirit. Secondly, it is hinted at in the words of administration: 'Preserve thy body and soul unto everlasting life.' And thirdly it is hinted at in the Prayer of Thanksgiving after Communion: 'And dost assure us thereby . . . that we are . . . *heirs through hope* of thy everlasting kingdom.'

(ii) ETHICAL EPISTLES:

1. *First example:* ADVENT 1: ROM. 13.8-14

The key passage in this exhortation is: 'Let us therefore cast off the works of darkness, and let us put on the armour of light.' The introduction of the terms 'darkness' and 'light' at this point lifts the whole exhortation to avoid various kinds of immoral behaviour above the level of mere moralism and links it with the *kerygma*. For the *kerygma* presents the coming of Christ as the dawning of the light (cf. Luke 1.78f.; II. Cor. 4.6). Those who have 'believed' (verse 11: the aorist suggests the concrete moment of Baptism) have accepted Christ as the light, as the dawning of deliverance from the darkness of the world around. Since their Baptism, the faces of Christians are turned towards the dawn, waiting for the sunrise of the Parousia which is drawing ever nearer (verse 11). This is the Advent situation. The behaviour of Christians must therefore be determined not by the darkness of the surrounding world in its separation from the light of Christ, but by the light whose coming the Church awaits. This means that their behaviour will be characterized by love (verse 12). Therefore, they must put on the 'armour of light' (ibid.), which is further defined as 'putting on the Lord Jesus Christ' (verse 14). This does not mean simply following the example of Jesus as an external moral standard, for that would still be the way of the law, and therefore the way of darkness. Rather, it means the

renewal of our baptismal incorporation into the Body of Christ.[1]
This is precisely what happens in the Eucharist, where we are
assured 'that we are very members incorporate in the mystical
body' of Christ. And having thus put on Christ anew, we are
enabled to fulfil the commandment of love, and to 'do all such
good works as God has prepared for us to walk in' (Prayer of
Thanksgiving). This is Advent ethics.

2. *Second example:* EASTER IV: JAS. 1.17-21

During the Great Forty Days the liturgical pericopae are
coloured by the thought of the presence of the recently baptized
at the services of the Church. For, as the reader will recall, it
was the custom in the early Church normally to baptize on Easter
Eve. It is natural therefore that the Epistles for these Sundays
should be selected from I Peter and James, both of which incorporate extensive material used in the instruction of catechumens
in the primitive Church,[2] while, in the view of many scholars,
I Peter[3] is actually an adaptation of an Easter homily addressed
to the newly baptized. These considerations should help the
preacher to link this Sunday's Epistle with the sacrament of
Baptism. 'Of his own will begat he us with the word of truth,
that we should be a kind of first-fruits of his creatures' (verse 18).
The 'word of truth' is the Gospel message of the redemptive
events in Jesus Christ, centred upon his death and resurrection,
the *kerygma*, which is dramatically enacted in Holy Baptism.[4]
Through this sacrament we have been made 'first-fruits of God's
creatures', the advanced guard of mankind destined to be summed
up in Christ as the Parousia (Eph. 1.10). The risen Christ is
himself described as the 'first-fruits' in I Cor. 15.23: we are the
first-fruits in virtue of our incorporation into his Body by sharing
his death and resurrection (Rom. 6.3ff.). It is as the first-fruits,

[1] See C. H. Dodd, *The Epistle to the Romans,* 1932, *ad loc.*
[2] See Philip Carrington, *The Primitive Christian Catechism,* 1940;
E. G. Selwyn, *The First Epistle of St Peter,* 1946, pp. 363-466.
[3] Cf. F. L. Cross, *I Peter, A Paschal Liturgy,* 1954.
[4] See W. F. Flemington, *The New Testament Doctrine of Baptism,* 1948,
p. 137.

the members of his Body, the advanced guard of redeemed humanity, that we are privileged in the liturgy to join already here and now with the 'angels and archangels and all the company of heaven' (the Preface) in singing the new song of the redeemed. But this 'is', this already existing privilege, carries with it an 'ought'. Just as the Jews emerged from the Exodus under obligation to the Mosaic law, so now Christians, as they emerge from the new Exodus of Christ's death and resurrection in the waters of Baptism, are under obligation to fulfil the demands of the new life—to 'lay apart all filthiness and superfluity of naughtiness'. This is precisely what we did symbolically in our Baptism, when we renounced 'the devil and all his works, the vain pomp and glory of the world, with all covetous desires of the same' (Public Baptism of Infants, *Book of Common Prayer*). But these renunciations, though accomplished once for all symbolically, have constantly to be renewed, as they are indeed renewed in the Confession and Absolution in the Communion service. But then comes also the positive demand: 'Receive with meekness the engrafted word which is able to save your souls' (verse 21). The word must not be preached and listened to, it must be 'received', assimilated into ourselves. Hence the 'ministry of the Word' culminates in the ministration of the sacrament, the visible Word. For the Word of God which is able to save our souls is not a statement or an abstraction, but an event and a person, Jesus Christ. Hence in the Prayer for the Church Militant here on earth we pray for 'this congregation here present', that they may not only 'hear', but also 'receive' God's holy Word, a reference, maybe, first to the sermon, but then also to the reception of the sacrament.

3. *Third example:* TRINITY XVII: EPHESIANS 4.1-6

This is an exhortation to unity within the Christian Church. But, as with the rest of the ethical teaching in the New Testament, the imperative is based firmly on an indicative. Behind the task of unity stands the reality of unity as an objective fact.

Despite the visible disunity of the Christian Church—with altar set up against altar and ministry against ministry, with the 'parties' and schools of thought within the separate communions, and with the tensions between individual members of a single congregation—there is an objective unity which is a given fact: there *is* 'one body and one Spirit, even as ye were called in one hope of your calling; one Lord, one faith, one Baptism' (verses 4f.). All this language recalls the sacrament of Christian initiation. For when we were baptized, we were brought, not into the Church of England, or the Methodist Church, or the Roman Catholic Church or the Presbyterian or Congregational Church, but into the Body of Christ, the eschatological community as it will be at the End. As members of this eschatological community which will be, we are one already. There is only one Christ, and therefore there can only be one Body of Christ. But the Church, though her existence is rooted in the eschatological future, has nevertheless to live in this present age. Hence she is exposed to all the disintegrating effects of human sin. Hence also the historical disunity which belies her eschatological oneness. Thus the unity of the Church, while it is an eschatological fact (verses 4-6), is also an inescapable task (verses 1-3).

It is now necessary to relate the two kinds of unity of which the Epistle speaks, to the liturgy. On the one hand, we start in this service at the point which we have reached in history, with that degree of unity and disunity which we already possess. Our eucharistic offering is the expression of that degree of unity which we already possess in history, of the unity between the members of the congregation there present, of the other local and world-wide churches with which we are in communion. Yet as we kneel at our separate altars and receive the same Christ in anticipation of his final coming when we shall all be one, we already experience a foretaste of that eschatological unity with those with whom we cannot at present be 'in communion' or united in history. That is why every Eucharist is accompanied by the heart-felt prayer for the realization in history of the given fact of eschatological unity: '. . . beseeching thee to inspire continually the universal Church with the spirit of truth, unity and concord: And grant that all they that do confess thy holy name may agree in the truth of thy holy Word, and live in unity and godly love' (Prayer for the Church Militant, *Book of Common Prayer*). At every Communion, as we kneel at the Lord's Table, we are meant to feel the pain of our scandalous divisions, of the lamentable fact that just down the road there are other Christians, also kneeling at the Lord's Table and receiving the same Christ, and yet unable to receive him with us or we with them—and then to come away with a new resolve to work for the reunion in history of Christ's Body which *is* eschatologically one.[1]

(b) THE GOSPELS

Despite the negative results of much Form Criticism,[2] it should not be overlooked that its more positive aspects not only help us to a more profound understanding of the nature and purpose of the four Gospels as theological documents, but—what has perhaps been less frequently noted—have a direct bearing

[1] The foregoing exposition is much indebted to W. Nicholls, *Ecumenism and Catholicity*, 1952, and to the essay by T. F. Torrance entitled 'Eschatology and the Eucharist' in *Intercommunion*, ed. Donald Baillie and John Marsh, 1952. I cannot, however, accept Dr Torrance's moving plea that the eschatological significance of the Eucharist not only justifies but demands the practice of intercommunion forthwith without tarrying for reunion. I have sought to do justice to the eschatological aspect of the Eucharist, which Dr Torrance rightly stresses, by insisting that the Church's eschatological unity is a recognized fact even as we kneel at our separate altars (for it is one and the same Christ who comes to all when the sacrament is duly administered according to his institution). But since the Eucharist is an offering in history of the memorial of the redemption, it can only be offered by those who are historically at one. Premature acts of intercommunion would not only induce a complacency with our present divisions such as would retard the achievement of historical unity, but would result in the false pretence to a unity which we do not at present possess in history. If we went back from the same Table to our separation and disunity in history, we should be eating and drinking judgement to ourselves as assuredly as we would if we were to partake of the sacrament without repenting effectively of our individual sins and purposing to amend our lives.

[2] For a recent appraisal of the positive gains of Form Criticism, see R. H. Lightfoot, *The Gospel Message of St Mark*, 1950, pp. 98-105.

upon the understanding of the Church's liturgical Gospels and of the treatment they require in liturgical preaching.

The Form Critics have likened each of the Synoptic Gospels to a string of beads. The string is the general outline of the ministry of Jesus prefacing the passion narratives. This means that as literary wholes the first three gospels are neither biographies nor histories, but *proclamation*. They were written 'from faith to faith'. The beads are a series of small self-contained units or pericopae. Before they were strung together they existed in oral tradition as isolated fragments, taking shape from their use in the manifold activities of the primitive Church, and in particular in the central activity of preaching. Thus each of the pericopae serve as illustrations of the central message of the *kerygma*. Each detachable unit proclaims the redemptive act of God in Christ in miniature. Now it is of the utmost importance to note that our liturgical Gospels are derived either from the 'string' or the 'beads' which go to make up the canonical Gospels. To the 'string' belong mainly the Gospels for the dominical feasts and fasts in the Christmas and Easter cycles.[1] The Gospels of the nativity cycle are prefaces to the *kerygma*, testifying to the transcendental origin of Christ, while the Gospels of the paschal cycle are parts of the *kerygma* itself. These Gospels hardly call for special treatment here, except to suggest that it should be the preacher's task to relate the specific kerygmatic event attested in the liturgical Gospel to the *kerygma* of the redemptive act of God in Christ as a whole. Take for instance the text for the Christmas Gospel: 'The Word was made flesh, and dwelt among us' (John 1.14). Too often one hears it handled in isolation from the *kerygma* as a whole, as though the Incarnation were detachable from the total event of redemption, to be treated as a jumping-off ground for some abstract philosophy of incarnationalism, or, in less exalted circles, for some ethical principle, such as humility.

[1] The Gospels referred to are as follows: (*a*) Nativity Cycle: Christmas Day, Christmas I, Circumcision, Epiphany, Purification, Annunciation; (*b*) Paschal Cycle: Palm Sunday to Easter Day inclusive, and Ascension Day.

This is to ignore the fact that the Incarnation is part of the totality of the movement of God to man in Jesus Christ. 'The Word became flesh' is God's initiation of a movement which is to culminate in the cross, the nadir of the divine condescension which is of a piece with Bethlehem.[1] That is why the climax of the Christmas festival is not the service of Nine Lessons and Carols, nor a pretty little devotion round the crib, but the Christ Mass, the Christmas celebration of the Holy Communion, in which we advance from the commemoration of the Messiah's birth in the Proper Preface to the rehearsal of his death in the Prayer of Consecration—a startling paradox to which Mr T. S. Eliot has called striking attention in Becket's sermon in *Murder in the Cathedral*:

> 'Dear children of God, my sermon this morning will be a very short one. I wish only that you should ponder and meditate the deep meaning and mystery of our masses of Christmas Day. For whenever Mass is said, we re-enact the Passion and Death of Our Lord; and on this Christmas Day we do this in celebration of His Birth. So that at the same moment we rejoice in His coming for the salvation of men, and offer again to God His Body and Blood in sacrifice, oblation and satisfaction for the sins of the whole world.'[2]

But the majority of the ordinary Sunday Gospels belong to the 'beads': they consist of separate pericopae. It would seem that the Church has always treated them as separate units, long before the Form Critics postulated their original separate

---

[1] One is tempted to think that the now widespread custom of kneeling for the *incarnatus* in the Nicene Creed and rising before the *crucifixus* is an unconscious reflection of this unbalanced theological emphasis. Cf. also a recent G.O.E. question (*Doctrine I*, March 1954): 'In recent Anglican writing there have been very few books from the "evangelical" side on the Incarnation, or from the "catholic" side on the Atonement.' If the view outlined in the text is the biblical one, it ought not to be possible for any conscientious preacher to deal with one doctrine in isolation from the other.

[2] *Op. cit.*, 1936 edition, p. 47.

existence in the oral tradition. Indeed, they may have been used precisely in the way in which they are used to-day, as liturgical lections before they were strung together in the canonical Gospels and their sources.[1] The three commonest forms of this type are the 'pronouncement stories' (to use Dr Vincent Taylor's convenient term), the miracle stories and the parables. The Sunday Gospels consist, for the period from Epiphany II to Lent IV inclusive, and for the Sundays after Trinity, of one or other of these types. The only other major class to be considered are the Johannine discourses, which provide the liturgical Gospels for the period from Easter II to Whitsunday inclusive. The Church had a profound insight when she treated these discourses as testimonies of the risen Christ pressed back into the incarnate life, thus anticipating the conclusions of modern criticism.[2]

In dealing with each of these types of pericope in the liturgical sermon it will be the preacher's task to relate the pericope to the *kerygma* which it proclaims, and then link it up with the liturgical action which is to follow. His first task is thus to penetrate behind the liturgical Gospel to the GOSPEL, the *euangelion*, the proclamation of the central event of Jesus Christ which it enshrines. Three examples of such treatment will now follow, the reader being reminded that these examples, like the treatment of the Epistles exemplified above, are not skeleton sermons, but illustrations of the preliminary theological spade-work.

1. *First example:* TRINITY III: LUKE 15.1-10. A PARABLE

Dr Hans Ehrenberg[3] has recalled a sermon which he heard delivered on this text on the Third Sunday after Trinity in an

---

[1] This is perhaps the element of truth in Dr Carrington's thesis in *The Primitive Christian Calendar*, 1952: the pericopae may have been used as separate lections in worship before they were combined together by the evangelists. But that is not to say that, as Dr Carrington holds, they were already arranged according to a calendrical scheme before they reached our evangelists.

[2] See, e.g., C. H. Dodd, *The Fourth Gospel*, 1953, pp. 397f.

[3] In a lecture entitled 'Still Higher Criticism', delivered in St Francis' Hall, Birmingham, in the early summer of 1943. It was subsequently published in a brief-lived periodical called *The Presbyter*.

English Cathedral about 1940. The preacher was obviously striving to keep close to the biblical text, rather than speak about a theme of his own choosing (what the Germans deprecatingly call *Themapredigt*) or impose his own opinions on the text. But he handled the parable of the Lost Sheep as though it were an illustration of the philosophical truth of 'the value of human personality'. Now this may or may not be a legitimate deduction from the Christian Gospel, but despite its appeal in the Anglo-Saxon world, it is quite irrelevant to the exegesis of the parable. And a sermon, as has been insisted throughout, is not a sermon in the strict sense of the term (as opposed to its loose sense of 'anything spoken in a pulpit') unless it is based on a sound exegesis of the text. If it be not this, the discourse, however learned, eloquent or edifying, is simply the proclamation of human opinion, and not testimony to the Word of God.—Now, as Dr C. H. Dodd and, more recently, Professor Joachim Jeremias, have insisted,[1] the parables of our Lord are never illustrations of general truths, or even of one general truth whether theological, philosophical or moral, but rather prophetic comment upon and interpretation of the concrete events and concrete situations in which the Central Figure is actually involved at the moment of utterance. The situation on which the parables of the Lost Sheep and the Lost Coin are offered as comment is indicated by verse 2: 'This man receiveth sinners and eateth with them.' In both parables, the shepherd or the woman is engaged in seeking something lost and rejoicing over its recovery. Then at the end comes the application: 'I say unto you, that even so there shall be joy in heaven (a reverential periphrasis for 'God shall rejoice') over one sinner that repenteth, more than over ninety and nine just persons, which need no repentance' (verse 7: cf. verse 10, where the phrase 'the presence of the angels of God' similarly means that God himself rejoices over the recovery of the lost). Jesus incurs hostile criticism for eating with publicans and sinners. The parables

[1] C. H. Dodd, *The Parables of the Kingdom*, 1944, pp. 11-26; J. Jeremias, *The Parables of Jesus*, 1954.

answer this criticism by furnishing a prophetic interpretation of the meaning of Jesus' action in eating in such doubtful company: God is seeking, saving and rejoicing over the recovery of that which was lost. The action of Jesus in sitting at table with the outcast is thus a prefigurement of the Messianic redemption to be wrought out on the cross, where the Good Shepherd lays down his life for the sheep (John 10.1ff.). Thus the parable, far from containing a comfortable truth about the value of human personality, sets forth the *kerygma* of the cross in all its rugged grandeur. Men are lost, and God descends to the lowest depths to seek and save them. It is thus to be noted that the 'green' Sundays after Trinity, so often regarded as dull and uninteresting, compared with the festival half of the Church's year, are in fact weekly festivals of the redemption. The Gospel of the Day sets forth the redemptive action of God, while the Lord's Supper commemorates that action before him and calls forth from him an act which makes that redemption a present reality. Our God is a God who seeks, a God who sought us in Christ and who still seeks us in the Holy Supper where Christ himself is the host who spreads his own banquet and sits down rejoicing to eat with sinners. This thought may be linked with the comfortable word in the liturgy, 'Come unto me all that travail and are heavy laden, and I will refresh you', as well as with the Prayer of Humble Access: 'We do not presume to come to this thy Table, O merciful Lord, trusting in our own righteousness, but in thy manifold and great mercies.'

2. *Second example:* TRINITY XXIII: MATT. 22.15-22 (a pronouncement story)

The climax of this incident, for the sake of which it is told, lies in the crashing pronouncement which comes in verse 21: 'Render therefore unto Caesar the things that are Caesar's; and unto God the things that are God's.' Jesus declares that in the reign of God which he has come to inaugurate there are things that are Caesar's and things that are God's. Behind this passage, therefore, lies the *kerygma* of the reign of God. But the things that are Caesar's are not therefore outside the realm of God or the kingdom of Christ, as though the state on the one hand could behave in absolute autonomy, while the Church, on the other hand, busied itself exclusively with 'religion'. Such a conclusion would be tantamount to a justification of political totalitarianism and of ecclesiastical pietism, and it is no accident that the two often walk hand in hand. Rather, there are things that are Caesar's because God himself has placed them in Caesar's hands, because Jesus, in whom God's sovereignty is asserted, has pronounced them to be Caesar's. The state is thus declared to be the sphere where God in Christ rules indirectly and mediately through Caesar, that is, through the officers of the state personified for us in Britain by the Queen. They are his *litourgoi* and *diakonoi* (Rom. 13.4, 6). It follows from this that the Church has to require from the state obedience, not to herself (that would be theocracy, against which the Reformation was a wholly legitimate protest), but to the commandments of God.

The things that are Caesar's are given to Caesar by God, and since this is so Caesar is responsible for administering his trust according to the will of God. This is expressed in the Prayer Book Communion Office when, after the recitation of the Ten Commandments we pray for the Queen. For it is by upholding the Ten Commandments as the pillars of society that the state acts as the minister of God ('that she, knowing whose minister she is', the first Collect for the Queen). And again, because God has entrusted the things of Caesar to Caesar, it is the duty of Christians and churchmen to render obedience to the state, not as though politics were a dirty business unconnected with or incapable of connection with the service of God—'that we, and all her subjects (duly considering whose authority she hath) may faithfully serve, honour, and humbly obey her'. We shall render unto God the things that are God's by offering our eucharistic homage ('It is very meet, right, and our bounden duty, that we should at all times and in all places give thanks unto thee . . .').

But at the same time the liturgy offers us an opportunity of rendering unto Caesar the things that are Caesar's by praying for all in authority as the 'Apostle' has bidden us (I Tim. 2.1): 'We beseech thee also to save all Christian Kings, Princes, and Governors; and specially thy servant ELIZABETH our Queen; that under her we may be godly and quietly governed: And grant unto her whole Council, and to all that are put in authority under her, that they may truly and indifferently minister justice, to the punishment of wickedness and vice, and to the maintenance of thy true religion and virtue.' Neither this language, nor the Collect for the Queen, are to be frivolously dismissed as Erastian or Tudor ideology. This is sound Biblical doctrine, as the Gospel of the Day shows. Thus the liturgy is our protection against totalitarian ideas of the state on the one hand, and against a pietistic withdrawal from it on the other. If the Prayer Book shows little encouragement for a 'natural theology', it does provide us with a theology of the natural order.

3. *Third example:* TRINITY XII: MARK 7.31-7 (a miracle story)

The Anglican preacher is often tempted to wander astray along a humanitarian bypath when he comes to deal with the healing miracles of our Lord. 'We are then left to suppose that our Lord was touched by the sight of suffering and that by the power of his faith he was enabled to alleviate the pain of certain cripples, and that a few more incidents of kind actions must therefore be added to the history of humanitarianism, and that the Church, if it be the Church of Christ, must be persuaded to undertake more seriously the support of doctors in their work of healing disease.'[1] Nowhere, perhaps, is this temptation so acute as on the Twelfth Sunday after Trinity: it is all too obvious to take the Gospel of the Day as an example of compassion for the deaf and dumb, and to concentrate attention on the efforts being made to relieve them and to appeal for their support. Of course, as

[1] E. C. Hoskyns, *Cambridge Sermons*, 1938, p. 58.

Hoskyns himself goes on to remark in a wider context, 'there is much truth in this'. This *may* be the ultimate application of the text, but only on the *other* side of the *euangelion* which it proclaims. For if we treat it as a humanitarian example we have not grasped the true exegesis of the text, and therefore cannot preach a real sermon. Now the clue to the meaning of this episode lies, in the subtle Markan manner, in the very rare Greek word translated 'had an impediment in his speech',[1] a word occurring in only one other place in the Greek Bible, viz. at Isa. 35.6. The reappearance of this word at Mark 7.32 is almost certainly deliberate: the evangelist is telling us that the healing of the deaf-mute is a fulfilment of the Old Testament prophecy concerning the Messianic age. It is a sign that the Messiah-designate has appeared, and is about to perform the ultimate Messianic miracle of redemption.[2] Like all the miracles in the Gospel tradition, the healing of the deaf-mute is a prefiguration of the Messianic salvation to be wrought out on the Cross. It is there that the ears of the deaf are opened to the word of God's forgiveness, and that the tongue of the dumb is opened to confess Jesus as Lord and to join in the song of the redeemed. Now this miracle is not merely an event of the dim and distant past: it becomes a present reality in the Holy Communion.[3] There the ears of men and women to-day are opened to hear the word of mercy: 'The Body of our Lord Jesus Christ, which was given for *thee*, preserve thy body and soul unto everlasting life.' There too the string of their tongues is loosed, and they can sing the praises of him who has done all things well, making both the deaf to hear and the dumb to speak: 'We praise thee, we bless thee, we give thanks to thee for thy great glory' (*Gloria in Excelsis*, sung appropriately in the Anglican rite *after* the Communion).

[1] E. C. Hoskyns and F. N. Davey, *The Riddle of the New Testament*, 1937, p. 167.

[2] Cf. my *Mission and Achievement of Jesus*, 1954, p. 42; Hoskyns and Davey, *op. cit.*, p. 120.

[3] Cf. the German distinction between *historisch* and *geschichtlich*, for which see my translator's preface to *Kerygma and Myth*, ed. H. W. Bartsch, 1953, p. xif.

All the miracle stories in the liturgical Gospels lend themselves to this kind of treatment. The preacher must pass from the particular miracle to the ultimate miracle of the Messianic redemption which it prefigures, and thence to its re-presentation by the act of God in the Holy Communion. For in the sacraments of the Church there is fulfilled the promise of the Johannine Christ: 'Verily, verily, I say unto you, he that believeth on me, the works that I do shall he do also; and greater works than these shall he do, because I go unto the Father.' For whereas the miracles of Jesus prefigure the Messianic salvation, the sacraments mediate it: Jesus has now 'gone to the Father'.[1]

(c) THE OLD TESTAMENT

At an earlier stage in the evolution of the Christian liturgy there were customarily three lections,[2] an extract from the Old Testament preceding the familiar Epistle and Gospel. The Old Testament lection has survived (rather than been substituted for the Epistle) at one or two places in the Book of Common Prayer, viz. Ash Wednesday, Monday and Tuesday before Easter, the Sunday next before Advent, the Purification and Annunciation of the Blessed Virgin Mary and the Nativity of St John the Baptist. Now the Churches of the Anglican communion, through their systematic reading of the Old Testament in the congregational offices of Morning and Evening Prayer, have probably familiarized their laity with the contents of the Old Testament more extensively than has any other part of the Church, Catholic, Orthodox or Reformed. And in the old days, when the Sunday morning service consisted of Mattins, Litany and Holy (or at least Ante-) Communion, it meant in effect that there was invariably an Old Testament lection in the liturgy. Yet we are in danger of allowing this noble heritage to slip away. First, the detachment of the celebration from Morning Prayer, accomplished

[1] John 14.12. Cf. my *Mission and Achievement of Jesus*, 1954, p. 43.
[2] J. H. Srawley, *The Early History of the Liturgy*, 1949, Second edition, p. 31, etc., also *Liturgy and Worship*, ed. W. K. Lowther Clarke, 1932, p. 374.

in most places in the latter half of the last century, has removed the Old Testament lesson and the psalmody from the same service as the Holy Communion. Secondly, through a complicated process of evolution during the past hundred years, there have grown up three different types of parish where the laity hear nothing at all or very little of the Old Testament, especially if they belong to the increasing army of 'oncers', who, if they attend in the morning, absent themselves in the evening. There are parishes where the laity attend an early celebration and then later in the morning attend a High or Sung Mass without communicants. There are parishes where the chief service of the day is the Parish Communion. And there are parishes where the principal service of the morning is Sung Mattins, at which it is by no means unknown (especially in the U.S.A.) for the service to be shortened by the omission of one lesson (and it is nearly always the Old Testament one which goes!) and a canticle, and by the reduction of the psalmody to the barest minimum. Whether designedly or not, the Anglican Communion is rapidly becoming Marcionite! In view of these modern developments and their accompanying dangers, it would seem imperative that future revisers of the *Book of Common Prayer* in every province should give serious attention to the provision of an Old Testament in the Communion service in addition to the Epistle and Gospel, thus not only meeting a modern need, but also returning to that primitive tradition which has always been professedly the norm of Anglican faith and practice.[1] If such a restoration were accomplished, the parish priest would find himself confronted with the need and opportunity of preaching a liturgical sermon on an Old Testament text more frequently than he does to-day. And since that opportunity exists already on seven occasions, three of which fall or may fall on a Sunday, it would seem proper at this point

---

[1] The Lutheran Churches, both Scandinavian and German, have met this need by a triennial system of lections, one series of which includes Old Testament pericopae. 'The Lambeth committee on the Book of Common Prayer recommend that future revisions should consider providing for an Old Testament lesson at the principal Eucharist on Sunday' (*The Lambeth Conference 1958*, 2.82).

to consider generally the problem of preaching on an Old Testament text.

It should be noted that our present Old Testament lections in the Prayer Book Communion service are taken from the prophetic sections of the Old Testament, and that the context of their use shows that they are understood as pointers to the redemption in Christ Jesus. This gives the clue to the way in which they are meant to be expounded in the liturgical sermon. *Jesus Christus in vetere testamento latet*. The preacher may indeed wonder whether such a view of the Old Testament can be sustained in face of modern historical and literary criticism. He may be tempted, if he preaches from the Old Testament at all, to handle it simply as the history of the religious development of Israel. But the preacher is not there to instruct the congregation in the history of religion, even of biblical religion. He is there to proclaim the Word of God, which is Jesus Christ. And unless he can use the Old Testament to that end he had better leave it alone altogether. Indeed, the modern decay of the belief that the Old Testament is in the last resort about Jesus Christ may account for its widespread neglect in preaching and its increasing disuse in liturgy. But such a view ignores the latest developments in Old Testament study. For although the traditional view that the Old Testament writers consciously and explicitly predict Jesus Christ, his coming and all the details of his life on earth has been generally abandoned, yet it nevertheless remains true that the Old Testament is an incomplete book, pointing forward to a future event which has not yet, from the perspective of the Old Testament, taken place. That event is the coming eschatological redemption, to which the Old Testament points forward by prophecy and type. This future is not announced clearly in all its delineaments after the manner of detailed historical forecast, but prophetically in the true sense of the word, that is indirectly, 'in divers fragmentary ways' (*polumerōs kai polutropōs*, Heb. 1.1). The encounter of Israel with Jahweh in the Old Testament is ever qualitatively incomplete, and carries with it the implication

45

of its ultimate fulfilment. Whatever is true will be.[1] Now the New Testament and the Christian Church look back upon the Old Testament from the standpoint of its fulfilment in Christ. The Christian has the missing clue to its understanding, for the event which still lay in the future when the Old Testament was compiled has now begun to come to pass since Jesus Christ came. It is therefore the preacher's business to lay bare the partial, fragmentary insights of the Old Testament in the light of their eventual fruition, always remembering that the Old Testament bears witness to a *logos incarnandus*, not to a *logos incarnatus*. Thus he will avoid the exaggerations of that pioneer in the revival of the Christological interpretation of the Old Testament, Dr Wilhelm Vischer,[2] who finds himself able to discover in the Book of Esther a complete theology of the Cross! Thus the preacher will confront the partial witness of the Old Testament promise with its fulfilment in Jesus Christ and relate that fulfilment to what happens in the Eucharist. In dealing with Old Testament prophecy, he will not hesitate to correct it in the light of its subsequent fulfilment. As Father Hebert has said:[3]

'The conceptions of the Old Testament writers are imperfect and incomplete, not only because of the imperfection which attaches to the human mind and its limited understanding, but also because the word which God was speaking through each of them was, as is stated in this verse of Hebrews (1.1), fragmentary and partial. The Messianic idea in its wholeness is complete and true, but it is only when the Messiah comes that it can be seen as a whole. When He has come, the contribution of each prophet can be seen as fitting into its place and as true in the context of the whole Biblical interpretation of His Person and His saving work and His Kingdom. But if

[1] Cf. John A. T. Robinson, *In the End God*, 1950, p. 37.

[2] In *Das Christuszeugnis des alten Testaments*, the first volume of which has been translated into English under the title of *The Witness of the Old Testament to Christ*. I am much indebted in this section to Professor Adolf Köberle's lectures in *Dogmatik I* at Tübingen in the Summer Semester of 1939.

[3] *The Throne of David*, 1941, p. 242.

we insist on taking the teaching of each writer separately, in isolation from the rest, and without reference to its Fulfilment, then it will be one-sided and erroneous.'

So much for prophecy. There is also the vexed question as to the use and limits of typology, which the preacher who grasps the nettle of Old Testament preaching is bound to have to face sooner or later. Here, however, his task is somewhat easier than that of the biblical theologian, since the preacher's material has already been selected for him by the Church, and he is therefore not free to wander—as the biblical theologian may be tempted to do—over the whole range of the Old Testament, looking for types. The Old Testament pericopae come to him with the imprimatur of the Church, and generally hallowed by centuries of traditional typological interpretation. This is notably the case with the lections at the daily offices during Holy Week, many of which offer types of the passion which have the sanction of the New Testament itself.[1] The preacher is surely on safe ground when he uses such types as these. Indeed, he would do well to confine himself rigorously to those Old Testament types which have the sanction of the New Testament itself. To quote Professor Lampe, 'The complex and impressive typological tradition of the early Church's liturgy is an excellent guide to the right use of typological exegesis, for the pattern of biblical history was enshrined in liturgy from a very early date.'[2] Outside the limits

---

[1] Wednesday Mattins: Num. 21.4-9: The Brazen Serpent. Cf. John 3.14.
  Evensong: Lev. 16.2-24: The Day of Atonement. Cf. Hebrews, *passim*.
Thursday Mattins: Exod. 24.1-11: The Blood of the Covenant. Cf. Mark 14.24; Heb. 9.20.
  Evensong: Exod. 16.2-15: The Manna. Cf. John 6.26-51; I Cor. 10.3.
(The revised Lectionary of 1955 has retained the Wednesday lessons, but substituted non-typological lessons on Thursday.)

[2] G. W. H. Lampe, 'Typological Exegesis' in *Theology*, June 1953, p. 205. The whole article should be consulted (pp. 201-8) as a warning to any preacher who desires to embark on the perilous seas of typology. Since the above was written there has also appeared *Essays in Typology*, 1957, by G. W. H. Lampe and K. J. Woollcombe.

set by the New Testament and the early liturgical tradition it is difficult to draw the line between legitimate and illegitimate typology. Above all, such a method of exegesis should never be used, as it has been used in some recent theological writing, to establish party or denominational opinion. Such opinions are entirely out of place in liturgical preaching, which, like the Prayer Book itself,[1] should confine itself to the central kerygmatic truths.

The preacher should further grasp clearly the fundamental distinction between typology and allegory. In typology both type and fulfilment are on the plane of history: the type belongs to an earlier date and points *forward* to its subsequent fulfilment. In allegory the figure which is interpreted has no independent historical existence of its own, but is merely a code for something else, and that something else is not a fulfilment on the plane of history but a timeless abstract truth. Thus Philo treats the patriarchs, not as historical (or legendary-historical) persons, but as symbols of various virtues. The real objection to allegory is that it gets away from the Biblical conception of God and his ways with men. For the God of the Bible is the God who deals with men in history, confronting them with demand and succour, judgement and redemption. He is not the ultimate Ideal or Absolute behind a hierarchy of values and virtues. Typology is based upon the conviction that God acts *consistently* in history, that his actions conform to a pattern because he is what he is. Hence his final redemption will conform to the pattern of the preliminary redemption in the Exodus. Typology therefore has its basis in Biblical theology, allegory in a non-Biblical philosophy.

[1] 'It (*sc. The Book of Common Prayer*) is my protection and the protection of the Church against Anglicanism and Evangelicalism and Romanism and Rationalism, and till these different devils cease to torment us, I will, with God's help, use this shield against them, whether other people prefer their party prayers or not.' F. D. Maurice, in his *Life* by his son, 1884, Vol. 1, p. 512.

Example: THE NATIVITY OF ST JOHN THE BAPTIST: THE
EPISTLE: ISA. 40.1-11

First, the preacher should begin by considering the literal, historical sense of the prophecy as intended by the author himself. The unknown prophet was speaking of Israel's return from exile in Babylon, and uses the story of the Exodus as a type of this new, and, he supposes, far greater deliverance (verses 3f.). This return will, he thinks, be the eschatological act of God, the revelation of his *glory* (verse 5), his eschatological coming (verse 10). This great event is being ushered in by the prophet, who in true prophetic self-effacement (surely an example for the liturgical preacher) describes himself as no more than a 'voice' (verse 6) preparing for the great event by announcing it. So much for historical meaning. But the return from exile was a disappointment: it did not prove to be the great eschatological event (see Ezra, Nehemiah, the first part of Zechariah, and Haggai!); Yahweh had not after all established his kingly rule among men. But his word cannot return unto him void, but must accomplish that for which he had sent it. Therefore the prophecies of Deutero-Isaiah were shelved for the future, thus becoming part of expectation of the Messianic age. At this point the New Testament steps in, announcing that the event to which the unknown prophet had looked forward has now begun to occur in Jesus Christ. It is in him that the 'glory' of the Lord is being revealed for all flesh to see. John the Baptist plays in relation to this event the same rôle as the prophet of the exile believed himself to be playing in relation to the return, the rôle of a 'voice'. This association of ideas may now be applied to the Church service. In the sermon the preacher is a 'voice', preparing the way of the Lord (cf. the Collect of Advent III, *Book of Common Prayer*). He announces the coming of Christ in his *glory*. This coming in glory, as an anticipation of the coming in glory at the *Parousia*, occurs as event in the sacrament of the altar. And then, after the event of the glory has been realized in the midst of the congregation, it acknowledges the event in the words of the *Gloria in Excelsis*, which in the Prayer Book rite forms the climax of the Eucharist: 'We give thanks to thee for thy great *glory*.'[1]

VIII. CONCLUSION: PRACTICAL CONSIDERATIONS

The Prayer Book, as we have already observed (see above, p. 14), requires by rubric a sermon to be preached at every celebration of the Lord's Supper. Rubrics have not the same binding character as statute law, and can fall by common consent into dissuetude. But everything possible should be done to secure obedience to this rubric at the principal Sunday service, when the congregation is assembled as *the* congregation, the local embodiment of the People of God. Where the principal service is the Parish Communion, there is comparatively little difficulty in executing the requirements of the rubric.[2] Where the principal service is the Sung Mass without communicants, the liturgical sermon is possible, but in a less satisfactory form. For the liturgical sermon announces the action of God which is to occur in and through the whole eucharistic action, including and

[1] The connexion of 'glory' with the Eucharist has an important bearing on the theology of the eucharistic presence. 'Glory' and 'presence' are closely related biblical terms denoting personal, dynamic activity on God's part. The Real Presence in the sacrament of the altar, however closely we choose to associate it with the consecrated elements, is not a static, thingly presence, but dynamic and redemptive, an event, an encounter between Christ and his Church. Reservation of the sacrament for the Communion of the Sick may be justified as postponed encounter. Devotions directed towards the reserved sacrament could only be justified as reminders of a previous event and encounter in communion. Celebrations of the Holy Communion at an altar where the sacrament is reserved and made the focus of devotional acts in the earlier part of the Communion service obscure the event character of the Eucharist.

[2] I say 'comparatively little', because the tradition of fasting communion (which I have no intention of belittling as a valuable personal discipline) does have the inevitable effect of reducing the sermon to a bare five minutes or so, and it is questionable whether there can be any really serious exposition of the Word of God in so short a time. Yet it is perhaps better to make the attempt than to eschew preaching at the Eucharist altogether.

culminating in the communion of the people. The reader will have noticed how frequently the divine action proclaimed in the scriptural lessons has been related in the foregoing meditations to the Communion as an anticipation of the *Parousia*. The preacher at a Mass without communicants finds himself in the embarrassing situation of pointing forward to an event which is not consummated at the service, but left suspended as it were in mid-air. A service of this type, however, is not only contrary to the express injunctions of the *Book of Common Prayer* and the main-stream of Anglican practice down to the present day, but is theologically wrong from every conceivable point of view. Fortunately it is being recognized as such even where it is still practised. Then there is the type of parish with the Victorian tradition of an early celebration followed by Sung Mattins with Sermon at a later hour in the morning. There are difficulties here of a different kind in the way of satisfactory liturgical preaching. Here the preaching of the Word tends to be completely divorced from the ministration of the sacrament.[1] One possible solution which has been tried in some places is to preach a brief parish communion type of sermon at the early celebration.[2] Another way of overcoming the difficulty is to regard the sermon after Morning Prayer as liturgically a part of the Sunday Eucharist which has already been celebrated some three hours earlier. In this case the liturgical reference of the sermon will have to be 'bent

[1] It is odd that 'evangelical' parishes should be so wedded to the Victorian High Church arrangement of the Sunday services, despite the insistence of the best 'evangelical' theologians that Word and Sacrament are complementary. 'The truth would seem to be that our Lord ordained both preaching and sacraments, and that they are complementary but not identical modes of his self-giving. Each is necessary and each has its special part to play' (*The Fulness of Christ*, 1950, p. 68). It would be interesting to compare the practice of pre-Tractarian evangelicals in this matter. One would have thought that Communion service (said, perhaps, with hymns) at 11 a.m. or 6.30 p.m. as the chief service of the day would be more in accordance with Evangelical principles than their present common usage.

[2] Cf. the kind of thing attempted for a College Chapel at Oxford by Austin Farrer in *The Crown of the Year*, 1953, also *Paragraphs for Sundays and Holy Days*, by D. M. Paton and J. T. Martin, 1957.

backwards' as it were to the sacramental event which has already taken place. This is perhaps not very satisfactory, but it seems to be the only way of avoiding what usually happens to the sermon preached after mid-morning Mattins, viz. that it gets dissolved into thin air, never leading to any responsive action on the part of the congregation, except the singing of a hymn and the placing of a coin in the collection plate. Sung Mattins and sermon is as much a torso as Sung Mass without communicants, perhaps even more so, as the latter does give opportunity for responsive action in the offering of a sacrifice, however mistakenly conceived.

Another matter which should be discussed is the relation of the 'sermon' preached commonly nowadays after Evensong on Sundays, or as it had better be called, the 'address'. Its sole rubrical justification lies in the injunction that 'the Curate of every Parish shall diligently upon Sundays and Holy Days, after the Second Lesson at Evening Prayer, openly in the Church examine children . . . in some part of this Catechism'. It would be a compliance with the spirit of this rubric, if not with the letter, which under present-day conditions is achieved in other ways, if the address after Evensong were of the nature of *instruction*, perhaps on some subject taken from the five-fold division of the Catechism.[1] It will be a great advantage to distinguish in this way between the 'sermon' proper and the instruction. It is a distinction which has its sanction in the New Testament differentiation between *kerygma* and *paraklesis* on the one hand and *didache* on the other (see above, p. 22). To begin with, there are many parish priests who complain of the burden of producing two 'sermons' each Sunday. Like Bishop Andrewes, they feel that if they have to preach twice they prate once. The Prayer Book, however, does not require two *sermons*, but one sermon, at the Eucharist, and, by implication at least, one *instruction* at

---

[1] (1) Church membership, (2) Christian Doctrine (the Apostles' Creed), (3) Christian Ethics (the Decalogue), (4) Prayer and Devotion (the Lord's Prayer), (5) The Sacraments.

Evening Prayer. Secondly, there is a widespread demand among the laity for more instruction, for 'definite Church teaching', and a certain dissatisfaction with pious exhortation. It is often suggested that this need should be met by the 'teaching sermon'. But teaching is not the direct and immediate aim of the sermon, properly understood. For the aim of the sermon is proclamation and the response of faith, whereas the aim of teaching is to secure understanding of the doctrinal, ethical and devotional implications involved in that response of faith. Teaching may of course be, and normally is, an indirect by-product of the sermon, but can never become its primary objective without so changing the character of the discourse that it ceases to be a 'sermon' in the proper sense of the word at all. Thirdly, the present shortage of clergy is compelling the Church to rely increasingly on the services of Readers. But it is highly questionable whether Readers should preach at all, in the strict sense of the word, or that the discourses they deliver should be called 'sermons' in the sense in which we have defined its nature. The Reader has no authority to preach the Word of God. For the authorized preacher of that Word is the Bishop (who was the preacher of the liturgical sermon in the early Church, as well as the celebrant), or in his absence, the presbyter who deputises for him. The ministry of the apostolic Word and of the dominical sacraments go together, and what God has joined together, man, even ecclesiastical man, has no right to put asunder.[1] Readers, therefore, should not preach 'sermons' in the technical sense—a fact which seems implicitly recognized in diocesan rules and in the new Canons (XCI), both of which forbid them to 'preach' at the Holy Communion, where, presumably, the only true preaching should take place. It would seem that the kind of address for Readers to deliver is an *instruction*, along the lines suggested above for the

[1] Note that the deacon may preach only if he be specially licensed thereto by the Bishop (fifth question in the Ordering of Deacons) and cf. also the rubric after the Nicene Creed in the Communion office: 'And nothing shall be proclaimed or published in the Church, during the time of Divine Service, but by the Minister.'

discourse at Evensong. Their function in the ministry of the word would therefore be somewhat analogous to those of a catechist in the mission field.[1] If, as seems most likely, it will be necessary to rely increasingly on their services in the future, especially in the countryside, they should be made responsible for maintaining the public offices of Morning and Evening Prayer and for the instruction of the faithful in the elements of Christian doctrine, ethics and devotion. For this a certain minimum standard of training in these subjects should suffice, comparable in kind, though more intensive in degree, to the training now given to Sunday School teachers. Preaching, in the sense in which it has been defined here, requires a definitely theological training, such as no Reader could normally hope to attain. It will then be necessary for the ordained ministers to visit these churches in order to preach the liturgical sermon, as well as to administer the sacraments. This is not of course to deny that certain lay persons will have the charisma of an evangelist, or even that of a prophet. These persons will be competent to deliver the type of sermon to be mentioned in the ensuing paragraph.

EVANGELISTIC PREACHING

A different kind of preaching is exercised in some churches, particularly, though not exclusively, in those of an 'evangelical' complexion. This is what may be called 'evangelistic' preaching. It is addressed to the outsider, aiming at 'decision' and 'conversion'. There is need for far more preaching of this type, as has been amply illustrated by the success of the campaigns conducted in many countries by the American evangelist, Dr Billy Graham. But it needs to be stressed that this is not the only type of preaching, and that it is in no sense a competitor to the kind of liturgical preaching which has been the subject of this essay. There are, as we have seen, three main types of ministry of the Word in the New Testament, *kerygma*, *paraklesis* and *didache* (see above,

[1] They could also read homilies if a new set were provided, which is much to be desired.

p. 22). Evangelistic preaching will clearly come under the heading of *kerygma*, and a church which bases its life on the New Testament will practise all three types of ministry. Secondly, it is doubtful whether the evangelistic type of preaching, addressed as it is to the unconverted outsider, ought to be appended to Sunday Evensong, as is often the case. For Evensong, like the other Prayer Book offices, is intended for the already converted. It is therefore unintelligible to the outsider, and when used as the prelude to evangelistic preaching is inevitably mangled or bowdlerized, a procedure which is fair neither to the liturgy itself nor to the potential convert.[1] Evangelistic preaching had best be accompanied by what French Roman Catholics call 'paraliturgy' or by no liturgy at all, as in open-air preaching. And such preaching may be attempted only by those who have the *charisma* of an evangelist, a *charisma* which is apparently independent of the possession of holy orders, and therefore to be exercised by all who have it, clerical or lay—'Quench not the Spirit'. Liturgical preaching, on the other hand, is the specific function of the ordained ministry.

Finally, something should be said about the celebration of the Holy Communion without a sermon. The writer has heard of a Roman Catholic priest in Germany who preaches at every Mass, on the ground that without the full ministry of the Word the Mass is incomplete. Such a procedure would certainly be fully justified by the rubric in the *Book of Common Prayer*. But we have agreed with Hooker that the reading of scripture may itself be a sufficient preaching of the Word of God (see above, p. 13). Moreover, the liturgical sermon preached on Sundays may be regarded as having an indirect relation to the weekday Eucharists, when there would be no sermon. For, as another Prayer Book rubric implies,[2] the weekday Eucharists are extensions as it were of the Sunday Eucharist. The faithful few who

[1] See G. W. Ireson, *Christian Worship and the Non-Churchgoer*, 1943, *passim*.

[2] 'Note that the Collect, Epistle, and Gospel appointed for the Sunday shall serve all the week after.'

attend a weekday celebration will normally have been present at the principal Sunday Eucharist, and will therefore have heard the liturgical sermon at which the Epistle or Gospel of the week was related to the *kerygma* and thence to its *anamnesis* in the liturgical action. The bare reading of the lections at a weekday celebration should therefore assist them in recalling their exposition in last Sunday's liturgical sermon, and thus enable them to apply the Word of God in the Epistle or Gospel to the liturgical action at the weekday service. The use of the Sunday propers during the week is, however, interrupted by the Red Letter Saints' Days and other Holy Days, and, where the provisions of the 1928 Book or elsewhere are used, by the Black Letter Saints' Days as well. Ideally, it would seem that a fresh liturgical sermon should be delivered on these occasions.[1] Where this is impracticable, a series of carefully chosen biddings at the Offertory should doubtless suffice, together with a Proper Preface, where authorized, as an expression of the *kerygma* contained in the lections and recalled in the Eucharist. As for the Black Letter Days, where they are observed, it is much to be desired that a reliable and concise 'hagiology' should be put forth by lawful authority. The relevant extract could then be read in place of the liturgical sermon.

IX. EPILOGUE

Every parish priest who contemplates the demands of the ministry of the Word must feel constrained to exclaim with the Apostle: 'Who is sufficient for these things?' It is easy to reply, 'Our sufficiency is of God.' But that reply can only rightly be made *after* we have put forth the utmost effort of our own. For the grace of God is always a paradox. Where men strive with all their might, there they can recognize in retrospect that it was

[1] This ought at least to be possible on occasions like Christmas Day, The Epiphany, Ash Wednesday, Ascension Day and All Saints' Day. On such days an evening celebration, desirable on other grounds, would make the liturgical sermon quite practicable.

'not I, but Christ in me'. The preacher's striving must take two forms, the one spiritual, the other intellectual. The focal point of his spiritual preparation to equip himself for his task will be his continuous identification of himself with the Word he is commissioned to proclaim as that Word is expressed in the Liturgy.[1] He must himself constantly live in the liturgy, in its daily round of the offices and frequent celebration of the Eucharist, in the yearly cycle of feast and fast. Thus will he learn to bring every thought into captivity to the obedience of Christ. His personal, private devotions will be not the occasion of the cultivation of his own soul, but will spring from the liturgy and lead back to the liturgy again. Thus he will make the liturgical scriptures the constant theme of his meditation. For his intellectual preparation he will strive to carry out his ordination vow to maintain that diligent reading of the scriptures and 'such studies as help to the knowledge of the same'. Such study may be linked with the liturgy no less than his private devotions. It is notable that most of the Fathers' commentaries on Holy Scripture were in fact their homilies delivered in the liturgy.[2] In the same way the liturgical preacher's study of scripture can follow the Church's lectionary, with its association of various books of the Bible with the different seasons of the year (e.g. Isaiah in Advent, Genesis and Exodus in Lent, Deuteronomy and Acts at Eastertide, and so on). At the other end of the communication line, he will be constantly moving in and out among his people, so that, like Great High Priest in whose name he preaches, he may be touched with the feeling of their infirmities. Only so can he hope to be used by God to proclaim his holy Word.

[1] See L. Bouyer, *Liturgical Piety*, 1955, especially Chapters 11 and 16. This book came to my notice after this essay had been written. It insists throughout on the integral relationship of Word and Sacrament along lines which often come very close to the lines adopted here, and is most welcome.

[2] Cf. J. A. Jungmann, *The Mass of the Roman Rite*, 1950, p. 398.

INDEXES

INDEX OF BIBLICAL REFERENCES

INDEX OF NAMES AND SUBJECTS

STUDIES IN MINISTRY AND WORSHIP

EDITORS: G. W. H. LAMPE & DAVID M. PATON

WHAT IS LITURGICAL PREACHING?

A

COMPASS

ROSE

Frankl   Nelson   Peale   Ungar

Published by DCN Publishing Co.

Copyright 2003 by Robert M. Nelson MD
All rights reserved

Inquiries should be addressed to

DCN Publishing Co.

Box 234

Harrington Park, NJ 07640

First Edition
1 2 3 4 5 6 7 8 9 10

Library of Congress Control Number: 2003090482

Printed in Indonesia

ISBN 0-9669196-1-0

Dedicated to
My Wife, Dorothy

" each of us has within a
force or setting that gives
our lives direction and focus"
Emerson

Preface

Ralph Waldo Emerson wrote that each of us has within a force or setting that gives our lives direction and focus. I have often reflected on this concept and wrote a short essay on the great influence my grandfather had on my life. It was titled "A Compass Rose", named after the nautical term for the circular disc or card with radiating lines representing a compass.

It then occurred to me to ask others to compose brief essays on those influences that have made their lives unique - especially from what sources or events did their lives gain direction and purpose.

The object of the series would be to inspire others to move in a positive and wholesome direction when confronted by today's destructive and negative influences.

I was fortunate to have Dr. Norman Vincent Peale contribute an essay. A memorable phone call to Dr. Viktor Frankl in Vienna, author of "Man's Search For Meaning", crystallized his essay. Finally, a contribution from the distinguished Rabbi Ungar completed the project.

It is my hope that many others will follow, especially some from the many admirable women in America and overseas.

Robert M. Nelson MD

CONTENTS

Robert M. Nelson, M.D.

Physician

Founder and President
The Meland Foundation

*T*he fishing seaport of Grimstad, on the Southern Coast of Norway, was a jewel of a village at the turn of the 20th century, alive and thriving with the activities of the day.

Two tall ships lay at anchor, their crews busily making them ready for their long journeys, and the fishing fleet was at the waterfront.

Housewives critically surveyed the bountiful catch while fishermen mended their nets in small sheds along the shore.

Close to the water's edge on the road called Storgaten (literally, "The Great Avenue"), named for its importance to the village, not its size, was the bakery owned by my *Bestefar* or grandfather, Baker Johnsen.

Surrounded by inviting sights and smells, villagers, sailors, and fishermen would gather for coffee, pastry, and conversation. They found much more.

Baker Johnsen's genial spirit overflowed with a love of people, a love of country, and a love of God, a spirit he shared warmly and without reservation.

Regrettably, *Bestefar's* generosity and friend-ship caused his financial downfall. Ships were permitted to secure provisions on credit. A "friend" who needed a note co-signed disap-peared. The bakery shop was sold to satisfy creditors. Baker Johnsen, without bitterness but with faith and hope in the future and God, set sail for America.

A new life awaited *Bestefar* and his family, but he did not forget the old. Years later, in 1936, he returned to Grimstad a local hero. He had voluntarily repaid every one of his creditors dollar for dollar what was due them.

After *Bestefar* and *Bestemor* came to America, it was my good fortune to share a home with them and my parents, a home I cherished until I was eighteen and went to college. During these years my grandparents were the center of influ-ence in the home, the neighborhood, and the church.

At the age of twelve an event occurred that changed my life. Near the end of the school year, each student in the seventh grade was given a Mantoux test.

Two days later the inner aspect of my right forearm was markedly swollen and tender.

About a week later, on returning from school, I noticed a letter in our mailbox. It was from the principal of the school and addressed to my parents. Not known in school for good behavior, I was sure this was another complaint.

Strong curiosity overcame ethical conduct. I went to the kitchen, turned on an old teapot, and waited what seemed like a long time for steam to form. I carefully steamed open the envelope and read:

> *"We regret to inform you that a Mantoux Test done on your son, Robert, indicates he has childhood tuberculosis."*

My heart sank. The event is as clear in my mind as though it were yesterday.

Although I knew nothing about childhood tuberculosis, the gravity of the letter suggested to me that I was going to die. Remarkably, in the weeks that followed, no one, physician or staff, sat down and explained to me in simple terms the significance of childhood tuberculosis, and the reasons to be optimistic about a cure. It seems to me that at that moment seeds were planted that would later develop into

The Meland Foundation

and the great need to give patients a full explanation of the health issues that impact their lives.

Almost overnight a boy who had been happy, nonchalant, spontaneous, and carefree became serious, introspective, and careful.

His bicycle, treasured and hand assembled from parts gathered from the neighborhood, lay unused. From the porch of the family cottage at Lake Lookover during that summer of prescribed bedrest, a boy once so full of life watched the other children boating and swimming.

However, the faith of my *Bestefar* – the faith nurtured in Norway and tested during his own trials – and the care given me by my parents lifted my spirit and helped dissolve my great anxiety. I found special comfort from my grandfather's favorite Psalms, the ninety-first and the twenty-third, that he often read to me in Norwegian.

Ps. 91:11

"Thi han skal give sine Engle befalling om dig, at de skal bevare dig paa alle dine veier."

"For He shall give His angels charge over thee, to keep thee in all thy ways."

Ps. 23:1

"Herren er min hyrde, mig fattes intet."

"The Lord is my shepherd; I shall not want."

Through my grandfather, I came to believe in God and His Son and to know for certain that His angels surround me. Through my grandfather a course was set for my life, a compass setting that has time and time again guided me in the right direction.

The Twenty-Third Psalm has been a Compass Rose and an inspiring influence in my life.

❖❖❖❖❖❖

SALME 23

Bestefar's Favoritt

*Herren er min hyrde,
mig fattes intet.*

*2 Han lar mig ligge i gronne
enger, han leder mig til
hvilens vann.*

*3 Han vederkveger min sjel,
han forer mig pa rettfer -
dighets stier for sitt navns
skyld.*

*4 Om jeg enn skulde vandre
i dodsskyggens dal,
frykter jeg ikke for ondt; for
du er med mig, din kjepp
og din stav de troster mig.*

*5 Du dekker bord for mig
like for mine fienders øine,
du salver mitt hode med
olje; mitt beger flyter over.*

*6 Bare godt og miskunnhet
skal efterjage mig alle
mitt livs dager, og jeg skal
bo i Herrens hus gjennem
lange tider.*

❖❖❖❖❖❖

PSALM 23

Grandfather's Favorite

*The Lord is my shepherd;
I shall not want.*

*2 He maketh me to lie down
in green pastures: He
leadeth me beside the still
waters.*

*3 He restoreth my soul; he
leadeth me in the paths
of righteousness for his
name's sake.*

*4 Yea, though I walk
through the valley of the
shadow of death, I will fear
no evil for thou art with
me; thy rod and thy staff
they comfort me.*

*5 Thou preparest a table
before me in the presence
of my enemies; thou anointest
my head with oil;
my cup runneth over.*

*6 Surely goodness and mercy
shall follow me all
the days of my life; and I will
dwell in the house of
the Lord for ever.*

❖❖❖❖❖❖

Biographical Sketch

Robert M. Nelson was born in 1920 and spent his early childhood years in Greenville, Jersey City, New Jersey.

A sense of pride, based on dedication and hard work, was evident in the Nelson family. His father was a carpenter and superb cabinet maker. His mother earned widespread admiration for creating life-like flowers from crepe paper. His grandfather was a master baker and his grandmother a skilled seamstress.

Robert spent hours watching his family at work. A child during the Great Depression, he was encouraged, like many others, to develop a sense of innovation and ingenuity. Thus, to have a bicycle he collected random parts and assembled them. Fortune smiled on him during his many journeys. The bicycle had no brakes and stopping consisted of placing the sole of the right foot between the front tire and the frame.

A bout of childhood tuberculosis at the age of twelve, described in "A Compass Rose", became an inspirational turning point in his life.

Robert M. Nelson was educated at Upsala College, where he was awarded the John Ericsson Fellowship in Science, and received his M.D. degree at The Jefferson Medical College. Together with his wife Dorothy, a registered nurse, his professional and family life has been centered in the Northern Valley of Bergen County, New Jersey. They have three sons and five grandchildren.

He has been an Attending Physician on the staff of The Englewood Hospital and Medical Center and is the president of The Meland Foundation, an organization he founded in 1980.

The Meland Foundation has a two-fold mission:

✦ To Provide Information on Medicine and Health to enable individuals to make wise decisions concerning their Health and Well-Being.

✦ To Distribute Literature to Build Hope and Courage.

In 1994 he was awarded the Bergen County Scout Award by The Bergen County Council of The Boy Scouts of America for his lifetime service to the community. In 1999 he was named Citizen of the Year by the Borough of Harrington Park in New Jersey and Clinician of the Year by the Health Sciences Library Association of New Jersey.

Viktor Frankl, M.D.

Psychiatrist - Neurologist

Author
Man's Search for Meaning

Man's Search for Meaning was named
one of the ten most influential books
in America in the 1991 Library of Congress
Book-of-the-month Club Survey
of Lifetime Readers

Deportation Train

Auschwitz

L et me recall that which was perhaps the deepest experience I had in the Concentration Camp. The odds of surviving the camp were no more than one in twenty-eight, as can easily be verified by exact statistics.

It did not even seem possible, let alone probable, that the manuscript of my first book, which I had hidden in my coat when I arrived at Auschwitz, would ever be rescued.

Thus I had to undergo and to overcome the loss of my mental child. And now it seemed as if nothing and no one would survive me, neither a physical nor a mental child of my own. So I found myself confronted with the question, whether under such circumstances my life was ultimately void of any meaning.

Not yet did I notice that an answer to this question, with which I was wrestling so passionately, was already in store for me, and that soon after this answer would be given to me.

This was the case when I had to surrender my clothes and in turn inherited the worn-out rags of an inmate who had been sent to the gas chamber immediately after his arrival at the Auschwitz railway station.

Instead of the many pages of my manuscript, I found in a pocket of the newly acquired coat one single page torn out of a Hebrew prayer book, containing the most important Jewish prayer, *Shema Yisrael*.

How should I have interpreted such a "coincidence" other than as a challenge to live my thoughts instead of merely putting them on paper

A bit later, I remember, it seemed to me that I would die in the near future. In this critical situation, however, my concern was different from that of most of my comrades.

Their question was, "Will we survive the camp? For, if not, all this suffering has no meaning."

The question that beset me was, "Has all this suffering, this dying around us, a meaning? For, if not, then ultimately there is no meaning to survival; for a life whose meaning depends upon such a happenstance - as whether one escapes or not - ultimately would not be worth living at all."

❖❖❖❖❖❖

Thus, the transitories of our existance in no way makes it meaningless. But it does constitute our responsibleness; for everything hinges upon our realizing the essentially transitory possibilities.

Man constantly makes his choice concerning the mass of present potentialities; which of these will be condemned to non-being and which will be actualized?

Which choice will be made an actuality once and forever, an immortal "footprint on the sands of time"? At any moment man must decide, for better or for worse, what will be the monument of his existance.

Henry Wadsworth Longfellow has expressed the essence of my philosophy in his memorable poem,

The Psalm of Life

❖❖❖❖❖❖❖❖❖❖❖❖

A PSALM OF LIFE

Henry Wadsworth Longfellow (1807-1882)

Tell me not, in mournful numbers,
*   Life is but an empty dream! —*
For the soul is dead that slumbers,
*   And things are not what they seem.*

Life is real! Life is earnest!
*   And the grave is not its goal.*
Dust thou art, to dust returnest,
*   Was not spoken of the soul.*

Not enjoyment, and not sorrow,
*   Is our destined end or way;*
But to act, that each to-morrow
*   Finds us farther than to-day.*

Art is long, and Time is fleeting,
*   And our hearts, though stout and brave,*
Still, like muffled drums, are beating
*   Funeral marches to the grave.*

In the world's broad field of battle,
In the bivouac of life,
Be not like dumb, driven cattle!
Be a hero in the strife!

Trust no Future, howe'er pleasant!
Let the dead Past bury its dead!
Act, — act in the living Present!
Heart within, and God o'erhead!

Lives of great men all remind us
We can make our lives sublime,
And, departing, leave behind us
Footprints on the sands of time;

Footprints, that perhaps another,
Sailing o'er life's solemn main,
A forlorn and shipwrecked brother,
Seeing shall take heart again.

Let us, then, be up and doing,
With a heart for any fate;
Still achieving, still pursuing,
Learn to labor and to wait.

❖❖❖❖❖❖❖❖❖❖❖❖❖

Biographical Sketch

Viktor Frankl (b. 1905) was born and educated in Vienna. He founded the Youth Advisement Centers there in 1928 and directed them until 1938. He was also on the staff at several clinics and hospitals.

From 1942 to 1945 Frankl was a prisoner in the German concentration camps at Auschwitz and Dachau, where his parents, brother, wife, and children died. Frankl vividly remembers his horrible experiences in these camps; yet he was able to use them in a constructive way and did not allow them to dampen his love and enthusiasm for life.

In the late 1940s he married Elleonara, with whom he lived in Austria. At the age of 80 he was still hiking in the Alps, and even remained active personally and professionally. He traveled all around the world giving lectures in Europe, Latin America, Southeast Asia, and The United States.

Frankl received his M.D. in 1930 and his PhD in 1949, both from the University of Vienna. Additionally he holds honorary doctorates from more than 120 universities around the world. He became Professor of Neurology and Psychiatry at the University of Vienna Medical School and later was a distinquished speaker at United States International University in San Diego. He was a visiting professor at Harvard, Stanford, and Southern Methodist Universities.

Frankl's works have been translated into more than 20 languages. He has had a major impact on the development of existential therapy. His compelling book "Man's Search for Meaning" has been a best-seller around the world.

This book was named one of the Ten Most Influential books in America in the 1991 Library of Congress Book-of-the-Month-Club "Survey of Lifetime Readers".

Dr. Frankl died in 1998.

Norman Vincent Peale

Pastor

Marble Collegiate Church

Author

"The Power of Positive Thinking"

*P*erhaps the most difficult problem I ever faced as a youth was my inferiority complex. I was shy and filled with self doubt. In fact, I lived like a scared rabbit. I constantly told myself that I had no brains, no ability, that I didn't amount to anything and never would.

Then I became aware that people were agreeing with me, for others unconsciously take you at your own self-appraisal.

One summer Sunday afternoon, when I was 12, my father said he wanted to call on a family living two miles out in the country and asked me to accompany him. As I look back, I am sure he wanted to find an opportunity to talk to me about my inferiority feelings.

My father's experience as a doctor, and his genius as a pastor, made him an acute curer of souls. His perception that abnormal guilt from bad thoughts, or wrong thinking, could be harmful made him adept in dealing with my inferiority complex.

We came to a place
where several trees had
been cut and sat on the
stumps.

Father described the mechanism of inferiority
feelings in a manner that would do credit to a
modern psychiatrist. He stated that scientific
treatment was not available in our village.

"But," he continued, "there is a doctor right
here who can cure any disease. He has a rare
and amazing power to purge our unhealthy
thought patterns. He can heal the sensitive
self-centeredness that lies at the root of
inferiority feelings."

Finally, Father asked me, "Norman, are you
willing to let this great doctor, Jesus Christ,
treat you? If you will let Jesus take charge of
your mind, indeed your whole life, you can be
freed of this misery which, if it continues, can
destroy your effectiveness."

I said I would
put my life into
the hands of
Jesus.

Father and I knelt by the stumps. I remember
that my dog, Tip, came up and licked my ear,
then sat beside me.

Father committed me to Christ in a moving
prayer.

He then asked me to tell Jesus that I was giving
myself into His hands and letting go, by an act
of affirmation, of all my inferiority feelings.

As we walked home in the gathering twilight, I
felt a sense of peace and happiness, as though I
was really on top of my problems.

Although I had another bout with inferiority feelings during my college days, the same remedy was applied again, with the result that this self-defeating thought pattern was healed through the positive power of Jesus Christ.

These experiences became the basis for my writing and speaking. They are the genesis of all the principles I have stated as

The Power of Positive Thinking

The key to my life's experience has been written in this passage from St. John — Chapter 1.

It is my Compass Rose.

❖❖❖❖❖❖❖❖❖

ST. JOHN

Chapter One

*In the beginning was the Word, and
The Word was with God, and the
Word was God.*

2　*The same was in the beginning with
God.*

3　*All things were made by Him, and
without Him was not any thing made
that was made.*

4　*In Him was life; and the life was the
light of men.*

5　*And the light shineth in darkness;
and the darkness comprehended it not.*

9　*That was the true Light, which
lighteth every man that cometh into the
world.*

10　*He was in the world, and the world
was made by Him, and the world knew
Him not.*

11　*He came unto His own, and His own
received Him not.*

12　*But as many as received Him, to
them gave He power to become the sons
of God, even to them that believe on His
name.*

❖❖❖❖❖❖❖❖

Born in the Ohio hamlet of
Bowersville on May 31, 1898,
Norman Vincent Peale was
the son of a physician turned
Methodist minister. He
authored 46 books, including
the all time inspirational best
seller,

The Power of Positive Thinking.

He was a motivational speaker on countless
platforms, the co-publisher of the world's leading
inspirational magazine, *Guideposts*, the
co-founder of the first school for pastoral
psychology, The Institutes of Religion and Health,
and for 52 years, the pastor of Marble Collegiate
Church in New York City.

Peale did not follow his father immediately into
the clergy. During a summer vacation he went to
a church meeting with his father where the
music and the sermon moved him deeply. Later
that year, he enrolled at Boston University
School of Theology.

Following ordination, Dr. Peale gained a
reputation as a dynamic pastor whose churches
grew.

At age 34, he accepted a call to Marble Collegiate Church in Manhattan. There he stayed, building the church through the Depression and World War II and into the early 1980's.

In 1933 he began a weekly radio broadcast, *The Art of Living*, which was to continue for a record setting 54 years. 1938 saw the founding of the innovative clinic for Christian psychotherapy, the Institutes of Religion and Health, and *Guideposts* magazine.

In 1952, Dr. Peale's fourth book was published in which, according to "Christianity Today" magazine: "He perfected his simplification of the Gospel message in the best selling *"The Power of Positive Thinking"*.

Peale, with his wife Ruth Stafford Peale, raised two daughters and a son. The family has grown to 8 grandchildren and 9 great grandchildren.

President Ronald Reagan wrote: "During my presidency, I had the privilege of recognizing Dr. Peale's achievements with The Presidential Medal of Freedom Award, the highest civilian honor of The United States Government."

He died on December 24, 1993 at the age of 95.

André Ungar, PhD

Rabbi
Temple Emanuel

As a small child — many years ago, many miles away — I suffered terribly with asthma. If I caught a cold, or if I ran too fast, I'd be clutched by this unseen cruel monster. For days on end, and through endless nights, I'd wheeze and cough and choke.

While other kids chased a ball and climbed trees, I had to watch from a window, confined to a room, a bed. Why was I so cursed? What had I done to deserve this dire punishment? I wept and wondered; I raged and rebelled. Nothing helped.

Yet as I look back, I owe that experience an immense amount. In retrospect, I believe it was a blessing, a gift, a privilege.

Why? Because it made me a bookworm, an addict of ideas, poetry, and beauty.

Why? Because it made me appreciate the kindness and care shown to me, and compelled me to feel a passionate sympathy with others who suffered. But most of all, because it taught me to experience the ecstasy of returning to good health. Eventually, the ordeal came to an end. I'd wake up once again able to breathe, fill my lungs with sweet air; I was alive, free, well, blissful.

Most people take breathing easily for granted. I could not. But in exchange for my agonies, I gained the rapturous delight of knowing with every fiber of my body and soul, what an extraordinary, miraculous thing every single breath is. What was - and is - trite and obvious and common-place to so many, remained forever a unique and priceless treasure to me.

Something pretty similar occurred to me in a somewhat different key, too. Growing up under tyrannies — Nazi first, Marxist later — in Eastern Europe, I later moved to Great Britain, and more recently still to the United States.

 Having groaned under the yoke of murderous bullies, I can savor the heady taste of freedom as, I daresay, few native born citizens of democracies ever can.

Likewise, having seen and heard and smelled war in my childhood, I can relish the all-too-often ignored glories of peace in a way closed to those who have never known anything else.

We take our families and friends all too easily for granted. They are familiar and, if not exactly contemptible, often almost boring. Only when a beloved person leaves us, or threatens to leave us, do we usually discover just how precious and central they are to our own existence. Like the air, like peace, like liberty, they are lightly shrugged away — but at what cost!

And finally, ultimately, eternally, the Presence of God: to remember it, to sense it, to commune with it, to be worthy of it, is surely the highest challenge to a truly human life.

The Psalmist captured this thought and my compass rose in the Hymn, The One-Hundred and Twenty-First Psalm, engraved on the wall of our synagogue.

אשא עיני

אֶשָּׂא עֵינַי אֶל הֶהָרִים   מֵאַיִן יָבֹא עֶזְרִי:

עֶזְרִי מֵעִם יְיָ   עֹשֵׂה שָׁמַיִם וָאָרֶץ:

אַל־יִתֵּן לַמּוֹט רַגְלֶךָ   אַל־יָנוּם שֹׁמְרֶךָ:

הִנֵּה לֹא־יָנוּם וְלֹא יִישָׁן   שׁוֹמֵר יִשְׂרָאֵל:

יְיָ שֹׁמְרֶךָ   יְיָ צִלְּךָ עַל־יַד יְמִינֶךָ:

יוֹמָם הַשֶּׁמֶשׁ לֹא־יַכֶּכָּה   וְיָרֵחַ בַּלָּיְלָה:

יְיָ יִשְׁמָרְךָ מִכָּל־רָע   יִשְׁמֹר אֶת־נַפְשֶׁךָ:

יְיָ יִשְׁמָר־צֵאתְךָ וּבוֹאֶךָ   מֵעַתָּה וְעַד־עוֹלָם:

❖❖❖❖❖❖❖❖❖❖❖

Psalm 121

Unto the hills I lift mine eyes,
Whence comes my help that lies in God,
Who is enthroned above the skies,
Who made the heavens and earth to be.

He guides thy foot o'er mountain steeps,
He slumbers not, thy soul He keeps;
Behold, He slumbers not nor sleeps,
Of Israel the guardian He.

He is thy rock, thy shield and stay,
On thy right hand a shade alway;
The sun ne'er smiteth thee by day,
The moon at night ne'er troubles thee.

The Lord will guard thy soul from sin,
Thy life from harm without, within,
Thy going out and coming in,
From this time forth eternally.

❖❖❖❖❖❖❖❖❖❖❖

Biographical Sketch

André Ungar was born in
Budapest, Hungary; sur-
vived World War Two in
hiding; moved to England
and received his higher
education there.

He earned his PhD degree in Modern Philosophy at the University of London in 1954. In
the same year, he was ordained as Rabbi by
the late Dr. Leo Baeck.

Congregations he has served include London's
historic West London Synagogue; Temple
Israel in Port Elizabeth, South Africa (until
his expulsion from that country, by an official
government order, for opposing apartheid);
and Temple Emanuel in Toronto, Canada.

Since 1961, he has served as Rabbi of Temple
Emanuel, located at 87 Overlook Drive,
Woodcliff Lake, New Jersey.

Over a period of two decades, he has taught at various American Universities, in the fields of philosophy, comparative religion and general Judaica. These institutions include New York University, the New School for Social Research and Hofstra University. For a number of years he was Chairman of the Hebraic Studies Dept. at Rutgers University in Newark, NJ.

Articles from his pen have appeared in numerous publications in this country and overseas. He has lectured from coast to coast (and beyond), broadcast on The Voice of America to lands beyond the Iron Curtain, and produced and narrated some forty television programs devoted to Jewish history.

Rabbi Ungar worked with the late Reverend Martin Luther King Jr. for civil rights; was involved in efforts to bring peace to Southeast as well as Southwest Asia, and participated in endeavors on behalf of Soviet Jewry. He has traveled all over Europe (East and West), Africa, Asia and the Americas.

He is married to Judy Bell, is the father of four children, and has eleven grandchildren.

Acknowledgements

Essay of Dr. Frankl— Personal Communication and Beacon Press. Permission granted to use this excerpt from "Man's Search For Meaning" by Viktor E. Frankl C. 1959, 1962, 1964, 1992 Published by Beacon Press, Boston.

Essay and Biographical Sketch of Dr. Norman Vincent Peale given by personal communication with Dr. Peale and The Peale Center.

Essay and Biographical Sketch of Rabbi André Ungar given by personal communication.

A special note of appreciation is given to Rev. Eric J. Fellman for his valuable encouragement of The Compass Rose Project.

The expertise and friendship of Frank Renfro in completing the publication of this volume is appreciated.

Illustrations by Wende and Harry Devlin

Graphic and book design by Dorothy C. Nelson

A Compass Rose is produced in co-operation with *The Meland Foundation.*

We would invite you

to write your own

Compass Rose

Please submit your essay and a biographical sketch to

The Meland Foundation

P.O.Box 234 Harrington Park, NJ 07640